P9-CFN-555

Ling-Ling
and Hsing-Hsing

Ling-Ling
and Hsing-Hsing

Year of the Panda

Larry R. Collins and James K. Page, Jr.

N F 2246

Anchor Press / Doubleday, Garden City, New York
1973

ISBN: 0-385-04803-3
Copyright © 1973 by Larry R. Collins and James K. Page, Jr.
Library of Congress Catalog Card Number 73-10535
All Rights Reserved
Printed in the United States of America
First Edition

To Stan Wayman

Contents

Preface

For many people, there is something uncannily "human" about giant pandas, even more so than those obvious relations of ours, the apes. No one has successfully explained this effect. It may have to do with the fact—equally unexplained—that pandas somehow are funny even when they are just sitting there doing nothing.

In any event, in their first year in the United States, Ling-Ling and Hsing-Hsing spent a good deal of the time asleep in their dens and that is *not* funny, especially for a visitor who has been standing in line outside the Panda House for a while to see them. (Most people, to be sure, are perfectly understanding that a lot of sleep is essential for the young, and as the pandas grow older they spend more time awake and active— and funny.) To an extent this book was written with those people in mind who got only a glimpse of black and white fur lying around a corner in a shadow. Mainly, this book is the low-down on the pandas' first year in Washington—a look at the antics of two clowns, a keeper's eye view of two truly extraordinary animals, their natures, and the methods used to provide for their well-being.

It may seem odd that a book written largely in the first person (that is, Collins) has two authors. In fact, this book has more like six authors. One of us (Collins) is a zoologist and has his hands full keeping track of the pandas as well as performing various other duties at the National Zoological Park. The second author (Page) is an editor for *Smithsonian* magazine. The four "silent" authors are the four keepers who comprised the original panda unit. All have a host of panda stories and we all enjoy sitting around listening and telling our own. After a while we even begin telling each other's stories. And that is really how this book got written.

Sources other than this book where readers may turn for panda lore are *Men and Pandas* by Ramona and Desmond Morris (McGraw-Hill Book Company, 1966), and *The World of the Giant Panda* by Richard Perry (Taplinger, 1969, Bantam Books, 1972). Both of these popularly written books were useful to us in preparing this volume, as were several more technical reports.

We should also point out that this book was made possible in the first place by Dr. Theodore Reed, who led the third U. S. expedition into the People's Republic of China and reappeared about a week later — as if by magic — with Hsing-Hsing and Ling-Ling. Our obligation to him is, of course, total.

Washington, D.C.   L.C.
April 1, 1973   J.K.P., JR.

Ling-Ling
and Hsing-Hsing

Mr. Lui, chairman of the committee in charge of the Peking Zoo, looked sad as the pandas were unloaded from a truck and placed on the plane that brought them to the United States. (Photograph by Theodore H. Reed)

1
P-Day

Nobody knows exactly when the giant pandas arrived in Washington.

Air Force records show that it was 5:45 A.M. when the early rays of the sun and a C-141 cargo plane arrived from opposite directions and met at Andrews Air Force Base in Maryland on April 16, 1972. The plane had flown straight through from Hawaii after a stopover at Guam en route from Peking. Though one of the first American flights to have originated in Peking in over twenty years, its arrival went largely unheralded. The press had not been invited and there was none of the fanfare with which President Nixon's party had been greeted two months earlier on his return from the People's Republic of China.

Instead, the few passengers were met by a small group that included officials from the State Department, members of the staff of the National Zoological Park and of the Smithsonian Institution including its Secretary, S. Dillon Ripley. There was some quiet though enthusiastic talk in the early morning chill while two large crates were off-loaded into a truck. They were light green lacquered crates and on each was inscribed, in both English and Chinese characters, the words: "Giant Panda presented from the Peking Municipal Revolutionary Committee. The People's Republic of China." No one at the base got much of a look at the sharp-eyed creatures peering from the crates at their new homeland.

A short while later, sometime after 7:30, a police escort led a small businesslike caravan up the blacktopped road that winds through the exhibits of the Smithsonian Institution's National Zoological Park. Still there were no newsmen or television cameras, no fanfare: just brief greetings and polite handshakes while the truck backed up to the front door of what had been, only days before, the Delicate Hoof Stock House Number One. Four bongos, rare African antelopes, had been relocated in a roomier paddock including a large pond, and two white rhinos that had lumbered around the building's outdoor paddock were now in crates themselves, on a truck headed west for the San Diego Zoo's breeding reserve at San Pasqual, California. The white rhino move had been planned several months earlier when zoo officials were considering ways of inducing the pair to breed.

The van doors opened and in the shadows I caught my first glimpse of the pandas—two black and white faces staring like mournful clowns through the black lacquered bars of the crate doors. Still in their crates, they were hoisted from the truck and placed, one after the other, on a scale. After subtracting the weight of the 227-pound crates, we found the female weighed 136 pounds; the male 74. I was introduced to Mr. Yang Cheng-fu, the chief panda keeper at the Peking Zoo, and the three other Chinese officials who had done the United States the honor of accompanying the pandas here. Together we inspected the hastily refurbished building that was now the Panda House.

Through an interpreter, we explained the layout of

4

the two separate enclosures, pointed out the thick glass walls, the air-conditioning system and the sliding doors with remote controls, and reviewed the procedures we had followed in cleaning — and cleaning again and again — the floors and walls. The Chinese were satisfied. It was time.

The female's crate was placed on the cement floor of her enclosure and keeper Tex Rowe opened the barred door. Immediately Ling-Ling exited and began to lumber around her new quarters in a rolling pigeon-toed gait, sniffing at the log chaise longue and the potted bamboo plants that had been installed only the day before. Finding her water pan, she sat down on her haunches, turned the pan upside down over her head and swatted it with her paw, sending it clattering across the room. The Chinese and Americans, watching from behind the pandaproof glass wall, were delighted to see the panda so active, though a few present thought some of her activity might indicate pique and not playfulness. Then we moved along the glass wall to witness the male emerge. The door of his crate was opened: Nothing happened.

Any child can confirm that five minutes is a fearfully long time if it is spent waiting and an interval of about five minutes became an eternity as we stared at the male's open crate through the glass. Then, slowly and gingerly, Hsing-Hsing emerged, cautiously and briefly examined his new surroundings, and took refuge out of sight in the small room that serves as his den. Thus it was that the difference in their personalities was established from the moment the pandas set foot on American soil. But everyone present was too busy, too excited, or, for a few minutes outside Hsing-Hsing's enclosure, too frustrated to note the exact time.

Diplomacy, lead, and a case of the sniffles

The two pandas had kept a large number of staff members of the National Zoo busy for several months already. And excited and occasionally frustrated.

Not long after President Nixon's announcement in the fall of 1971 that he would make the first Presidential visit to China in American history, the zoo's director, Dr. Theodore Reed, asked me to prepare a "work-up" on giant pandas — to learn all I could about pandas in the wild and in captivity. In hindsight, one might wonder if Dr. Reed had been forewarned, but he had no advance knowledge of the coming events and was, at this stage, working only from the shrewdness and sophistication one learns as director of the nation's zoo, located some six miles north of the White House.

As it turned out, not a great deal was known about giant pandas — at least outside China, the only place they exist in the wild. For so universally popular an animal, it is surprising that so little scientific knowledge existed for me to "work up" until you remember that only seventeen live giant pandas had ever been brought to Western countries. Giant pandas are one of the few animals known by so few specimens that they are referred to by their personal, humanly endowed name even in formal scientific treatises. A large amount of zoological information was either lacking or contradictory. There was even great disagreement on the basic question of what kind of animal the giant panda is.

As the weeks passed, most of the world speculated about the implications of President Nixon's China visit for international relations and the pursuit of peace. At the zoo, speculation flourished, despite Dr. Reed's caveats, that a panda would be coming to the United States. Then, while the President was in China in February, we along with the rest of the world heard Chou En-lai's announcement that the People's Republic of China did indeed intend to make a zoological gift to the people of the United States — of *two* pandas. It was also announced that the United States would deliver to Peking two musk oxen, arctic animals which the Peking Zoo lacked and especially coveted.

Immediately the major zoos of the United States began to argue their briefs. The Bronx Zoo in New York had maintained the greatest number of pandas (4) and the Brookfield Zoo in Chicago had had the most recent experience with pandas; the last of its animals had died in 1953 and their expert panda keeper, Leroy Woodruff, was still employed there. Philadelphia, New York, St. Louis, San Diego, and many other zoos pressed their claims persuasively. Nonetheless it seemed likely to the staff in Washington that the pandas would come to the National Zoological Park, traditionally the home for such gifts of state. Among the fruits of diplomacy already in residence were a pair of Komodo dragons from Indonesia, red kangaroos presented by Australia, an elephant from Africa and two from India, pygmy hippos from Liberia, an Indian rhino, one lesser panda, and kiwis from New Zealand.

On Monday, March 12, 1972, the White House finally did make its decision public. (Like everyone else, we heard of it only when we read it in the newspapers.) The announcement launched a frenzy of activity which came to be known as pandamonium. We had only weeks and little information to prepare a suitable home for the animals, to select and train keepers, and to make the hundreds of decisions and delicate arrangements necessary for so important a matter of state as well as zoology. It was unknown, for example, until a few days before their arrival, what sex and age the pandas would be. Hopes for future panda progeny sank when local newspapers published rumors that one was a near infant, the other a fifteen-year-old (which, among pandas, means the golden years).

On February 22, several of us met in Dr. Reed's office to pick the pandas' quarters. We discussed using two cages in the great-ape section of the Apes and Small Mammals House, but it has to be warm in there for the apes, and pandas, whose natural habitat is high in the wet, snowy mountains of western China, like it cold. We thought of renting temporarily a large semitractor-trailer truck, the kind circuses use to house and haul their animals, but a call to Florida turned up the fact that none was available. In either of these cases, too, there would have been a security problem: not only would large crowds of people have to be accommodated and kept away from the pandas, but the pandas would have to be kept away from the people. Pandas look cuddly but, as Dr. Reed explained in a press conference shortly after they arrived, "They can knock the hell out of you."

We decided finally to use the home of the bongos and

the rhinos because it was air conditioned, and its layout permitted a glass wall to be installed and other security measures to be taken. Also, there we could handle the huge crowds we knew would be on hand from the first day.

The expected crowds were also a determinant in selecting keepers. Not only did these men have to be thoroughly versed in handling animals and willing to "go the extra mile" — these would, after all, be the two most important animals in the United States — but the keepers would require a fine sense of public relations: they would need the patience to answer the same questions a hundred or more times a day. Not surprisingly, twenty-two keepers at the zoo volunteered for this duty and ultimately we selected four men: Tex Rowe, an older man with years of animal experience in zoos, circuses, and carnivals; Mike Johnson, a short, burly young keeper from the Reptile House; Curley Harper, who had worked in most of the zoo's exhibits; and David Bryan, who had previously cared for the bongos and white rhinos.

Their training began immediately, as did work on the new panda house. And our quest for panda lore quickened. Leroy Woodruff flew in from Chicago to talk to our keepers. At the last minute, I was dispatched to London to get firsthand information about Chi-Chi, the female at the London Zoo. There, in the care of Chi-Chi's keeper, Sam Morton, I saw my first live panda. She was fifteen years old then and very inactive, having already had her great days repelling the advances of An-An of Moscow during two unsuccessful attempts at an arranged marriage. Chi-Chi, it seems, preferred Sam Morton and other human friends. Most of the day that I spent there, she remained in her den. (Not long afterward, on July 22, 1972, Chi-Chi died peacefully in her sleep, the victim of an apparent heart attack. Then, only months later, on October 15, her frustrated suitor of old also succumbed in Moscow.) At London, I gathered as much information as I could, for the most part details such as how high the walls should eventually be in our outdoor panda pens. Though seemingly mundane, such considerations are at the heart of the matter, as we learned later.

Not only did we need all the information we could scratch together, a panda house, and trained keepers; we needed bamboo. And, happily, there were several stands of suitable bamboo growing right in the zoo. Indeed we found ourselves in the opposite position of many local gardeners who, having planted bamboo in their backyards, are distressed to find it coming up through their brick terraces and sending shoots up under the foundations of their houses. For such people, bamboo can quickly become an anathema, a haunting reminder that the jungle will take over after, and maybe before, we have gone from the earth. For us at the zoo, bamboo is welcome almost anywhere it grows. We soon became bamboo freaks, encouraging our existing stands, sending horticulturalists on the staff into almost every available corner and cranny of the zoo grounds to plant more. John Monday, the grounds foreman, was sent on a three-day trip south to hunt up additional sources. Yet there was an important precaution to be taken here as well.

The air of most urban areas contains increasingly high levels of lead, the result largely of lead molecules pouring forth from the exhaust pipes of thousands upon thousands of cars. This lead can concentrate in the tissues of plants and animals including man and, above certain levels, it is well known to be highly toxic. Recent studies had shown that grass and shrubs along highways had dangerous levels of lead. It was possible that even the bamboo stands at the National Zoo, though it is tucked away in the hills and gorges of Rock Creek Park, might be sufficiently contaminated to be dangerous.

While I was in London, Dr. Reed ordered the bamboo tested for lead content, and there was a momentary scare when the District of Columbia Public Health Department and scientists at the zoo found very high lead levels in one of our bamboo stands. The other stands, however, proved so low in lead that it was impossible to make accurate measurements, meaning that they were far below the toxic level. And, in continuing checks, the dangerous bamboo stand has since been found to be as low as the others, leading us to believe that the first alarming reading was some momentary and unexplained form of contamination.

As all of this activity took place and pandas filled our minds all day every day, rumors began to circulate about the date of the pandas' arrival. For example, on March 2, Dr. Reed and I spent the afternoon with the sister of a man well known in the annals of pandas: Tangier Smith. The most famous and one of the most successful animal trappers who explored the remote reaches of Asia in the 1920s and 1930s in pursuit of exotic wildlife, Tangier Smith had sent three live giant pandas to zoos in the United States and Europe. Sometimes, according to his sister who just happened to be in town for the day, these exports were accomplished by transporting the animals in caravans of empty oil trucks.

When Dr. Reed and I returned to the zoo late that afternoon, we found an entire NBC television news crew camped out at the Elephant House, just down the hill from where construction had begun (but which was by no means complete) on the improvements for the new Panda House. The journalists said they had word the pandas were due any minute. Dr. Reed said that they were not due that day and the journalists might as well go home. The journalists said they were absolutely certain that their source was reliable and would it be all right if they waited, just in case. (They stayed most of the night.) So certain were they that Dr. Reed and I began to wonder if NBC knew something we didn't, and we had a few panicky moments wondering where in the world we would put two pandas if they did show up.

While such rumors bubbled and while serious preparations went forward, the day finally came for Dr. Reed to fly to San Francisco where he would pick up two musk oxen from the zoo there and fly to Peking. His trip, it turned out, was postponed by a head cold. Milton, the shaggy young male musk ox, had a bad case of the sniffles, making it impossible for him to undertake so strenuous a journey. For two weeks, Milton's plight made him the first musk ox to have ever received widespread sympathy from the American public. He became a minor favorite of the press and some people wondered if Milton's cold was not a psychosomatic sign that he did not want to go to China (though one also heard talk that musk oxen were not really a sufficiently elegant gift if you compared them to so exciting a pair of animals as giant pandas).

When Milton had recuperated enough to travel he and the rather ignored Matilda, a young female, boarded the C-141 cargo plane for China on April 6, along with Dr. Reed, Day O. Mount of the State Department, and the flight crew. Ten days later the plane returned, putting to rest the rumors about arrival date, aged pandas, and whatnot.

Yet, like water seeking its level, Washington requires a new rumor to replace old ones. Word followed the pandas from Peking to the effect that no sooner had a still-sniffling Milton been whisked from the airport to the Peking Zoo than his hair began to fall out, certainly a threatening blow to American-Chinese relations. This rumor proved to be substantially true, though not a cause for alarm among diplomats: Both musk oxen were in their normal molting period and their winter coats were indeed falling out, giving them a scruffy appearance which by no means dampened the enthusiasm of countless zoo visitors who flocked to the Peking Zoo to see them only a day after their arrival.

Sleeping giants

Finally Ling-Ling and Hsing-Hsing (pronounced Shing-Shing) were among us. Minutes after they emerged from their light green crates, the four keepers and I joined Ma Yung, one of the Chinese zoologists, in the kitchen adjoining the panda enclosures where he prepared a meal of rice gruel, corn meal, milk, apples, and carrots. Both pandas took eagerly to this, their first meal in America, and to their second meal later on in the afternoon. Ling-Ling finished her breakfast with what had already become a characteristic gesture: Once every morsel was gone she turned her pan upside down over her head. Between meals, the pandas explored their enclosures but for the most part they slept, Hsing-Hsing in the shadowed recesses of his den.

We kept the animals under wraps for four days until Thursday, April 20, when Mr. Ting Hung, a high-ranking official of the Peking Government, formally presented them to the people of the United States and was thanked in return by Mrs. Nixon at a brief ceremony outside the Panda House. The ceremony at an end, the invited dignitaries went inside, eagerly pursued by the press corps who were getting their first look at the pandas. With no appreciation whatsoever for so historic a moment, Hsing-Hsing was asleep, a bundle of black and white fur barely visible in his den. Ling-Ling, on the other hand, was much in evidence — and she was brown and black. A few days before, she had begun her demolition exercises on the potted bamboo in her enclosure, tearing off stems, eating some, and leaving the rest strewn about the cement floor. The unusual coloration she presented to Mrs. Nixon was the result of three days of doing headstands in the bamboo pots. And for this elegant assemblage on Thursday morning she performed one of her water pan tricks, holding it up to her face and tipping it higher and higher until she rolled over backward, the pan still clutched to her face . . . and, it seemed to me, one eye on the crowd.

Even so, her exuberance was a sometime thing during

From the outset, Ling-Ling was curious and bold. Here she explores her log pile in April. (Photograph by Don Carl Steffen)

her first days at the zoo. Both animals slept most of the time, Hsing-Hsing so much that Mr. Yang expressed alarm. Perhaps the male would not adapt to his new surroundings and his new keepers with their different uniforms, their different voices and odors. We had decided before the pandas' arrival that the keepers would maintain a round-the-clock watch for the first few days and, as a result, we were able to assure Mr. Yang that the problem was not the new surroundings but a complication of the jet age. It seemed that the pandas were still on Peking time. Both were active at night; Ling-Ling was more so but even Hsing-Hsing would make nocturnal patrols of his enclosure and climb on the logs of his chaise longue.

After the formal presentation, the Panda House was opened to the public and thousands lined up. The following day, the four Chinese began their long journey home via New York City, and the lines continued to form outside the Panda House. On Saturday, April 22, it rained in torrents and the line wound around the now-barren paddock where the white rhinos had lived, down the sloping, tree-lined path all the way to the old stone Elephant House. And unless it happened to be feeding time, at 9:30 A.M. and 4:00 P.M., when the pandas could be coaxed from their dens, these two greatest tourist attractions in a city glutted with historic monuments and memorials, these two most celebrated animals in the world, the first tangible evidence of President Nixon's opening to China, Ling-Ling and Hsing-Hsing, slept peacefully.

Hsing-Hsing, the male, was shy and reserved. When he wasn't asleep, his early days were spent quietly. The bamboo pots were a kind of refuge. (Photograph by Don Carl Steffen)

Ling-Ling. (Photograph by Stan Wayman)

2
Caution

I'd rather tangle with a bull crocodile or wrestle a bear than mess around with *that* clown.

— MIKE JOHNSON

It all happened very quickly, as such things do. For several days the keepers and the two pandas had been settling down to a routine. The pandas were at their most active during and for a while after mealtimes, and except to clean out their enclosures every morning and feed them twice a day, there was little reason for us to enter. We wanted as few disturbances as possible for the pandas so that they could accustom themselves to their new surroundings. One or two professional photographers connected with the Smithsonian Institution were permitted inside briefly because the laminated glass played havoc with color film but, as is still the case, only the keepers went in regularly and even this was kept to a minimum.

On the thirteenth day after their arrival, Mike Johnson opened the door between Ling-Ling's den and her enclosure and walked in carrying a pan of rice gruel. The female was lying on the other side of her enclosure and as usual watched the keeper closely as he went over in front of the log pile and set the pan down. When he straightened up and looked back at Ling-Ling, it was almost too late. She was just about on him.

Reflexively, Mike stiff-armed the onrushing panda, his hand on her broad forehead, and pushed her head down to the floor—enough of a diversion for him to have time to duck around between the logs and the wall.

Immediately Ling-Ling was on the logs facing him, her head lowered. Mike feinted left and Ling-Ling parried. Then to the right—parry, feint, parry, in the classic manner.

"I knew she wasn't going to jump," said Mike afterward. "Don't ask me why. I just knew she wasn't going to come down off those logs on me."

Finally Mike slipped out from behind the logs to a position behind a bamboo pot. This proved to be little refuge. Ling-Ling charged and around and around the bamboo pot they ran until Dave Bryan, who was also on duty at the time, got to the den door and opened it as a breathless Mike Johnson bolted through.

Clearly one had to be careful of Ling-Ling. It was too early for us to know if she was being aggressively hostile or just playful, but whatever the motivation, caution was obviously in order. Hsing-Hsing, on the other hand, was altogether less threatening. On several occasions in the first few weeks, he lumbered purposefully toward a keeper—and the keeper would retreat—but the panda never made a sudden lunge. Indeed, one time Mike Johnson almost absent-mindedly held out a carrot and he quietly took it, sat down, and ate it.

To hold out a carrot to Ling-Ling, however, was to invite a flash of violence. She bats such an object—and has many times—with the blinding speed of Muhammed Ali in his prime. (Later, of course, she retrieves it from across the enclosure and eats it.) Not only can Ling-Ling strike quickly but she is extraordinarily fleet of foot as we, and particularly Tex Rowe, learned not too many days after Mike Johnson's experience.

The dancing keeper

Dave Bryan and I were outside the glass wall with the visiting crowd when we heard someone shout, "Oh, look! He's playing with her!"

"Oh, my God," groaned Dave as we turned to look through the glass. Tex had entered her enclosure with her food and, keeping a wary eye on the panda, assumed he was safe since she was reclining across the room from him. But in a split second she was on him and had forced him against the wall in a corner. A potted bamboo hemmed him in on his third side and Ling-Ling was in front of him. With the unique grasping paw that pandas possess (see page 126), Ling-Ling had grabbed him just under his right knee and attempted to sink her teeth into his left leg.

Tex recalled later that once he realized her teeth had bitten through only his cowboy boot, missing his ankle-bone, he ceased to be scared and concentrated on keeping his left leg wiggling so that she could not get a good shot at it.

"So I danced," says Tex. "She had a hold of my right leg with her hand and I just kept kicking and waving my left. I was dancing. I'll tell you. The people out there thought I was dancing too."

At this point Curley Harper darted into the enclosure, grabbed Ling-Ling's haunches in his hands, and pulled her off Tex. She went for Curley and that was just enough of a distraction for Tex to escape through the side door. Meanwhile I had been trying to get into the den from the public area and was having a frustrating bout with several keys on my chain. Dave Bryan, having an extremely fast draw with the necessary passkey, opened the door. We found that Tex was already out of the enclosure via a different door which was shut behind him. But Curley was still in there, I thought, with a sinking feeling in my chest; he would surely be torn apart.

Both men still guffaw over my reaction when we recall the incident, and Tex will say, "Curley, there, he's fast as a bullet when he needs to be. He got old Ling off me and then he left so fast I didn't see him go by either."

"It was splitsville," agrees Curley.

Several weeks afterward, when someone happened to ask Tex how many claws there are on a panda's foot, he hiked up his right trouser leg to the knee and said, "Well, let's see. One, two, three . . ."

Chinese interpretations

Ling-Ling means "cute little girl," the Chinese told us. And except for those visitors who happened to witness her two attacks (and even for some of them!), the name was apt. She continued to be the clown, the charmer, batting her food dish around the enclosure, taking up absurd positions in the bamboo pots, and every now and then approaching the glass wall and swatting it as if to signal to the audience on the other side that she was ready to play. As a crowd-pleaser,

Ling-Ling almost completely eclipsed the male, whose name means "bright star." Hsing-Hsing would have to wait until he grew up a little before he achieved his fair share of stardom. In the early weeks he continued to be mild-mannered and reserved, spending most of his time in his den.

Before their departure for New York, the Chinese officials, who had accompanied Ling-Ling and Hsing-Hsing to this country, had given us a considerable amount of information about the care and breeding of captive pandas. Among other things they told us that the males are the rambunctious ones while females are generally more retiring and easygoing. They had warned us to be particularly careful of Hsing-Hsing because he was known to bite.

If that was the rule then our pandas were the exceptions that proved it. Perhaps the discrepancy was due to nothing more than individual character differences. After all, anyone who has spent much time studying the behavior of animals knows that textbook descriptions are good only up to a point: individual personalities can differ among pandas as well as humans.

On the other hand, a few people hinted darkly, perhaps the Chinese had mixed them up in transit. Maybe Ling-Ling was really Hsing-Hsing the male and vice versa. The mind reeled with the international implications. After all, Mei-Mei, who had lived in the Brookfield Zoo in Chicago for four and a half years, was thought to be a female. It was only when "she" died that chagrined zoologists discovered that Mei-Mei was a male. This is not as absurd as it sounds. The world's most famous gorilla, Gargantua, was discovered to be a female only when he — rather, she — died and an autopsy was performed. As in many animals, the genitalia of giant pandas are small and well obscured, with the male's testes being internal in position; even close examination of a live animal by an expert biologist can be inconclusive. Nonetheless, we felt perfectly confident about the Chinese zoologists assay of the sex of our two pandas because they have had considerably more experience with giant pandas than Western zoologists. In addition our two animals were beginning to exhibit sharply contrasting behavioral characteristics, especially when they began marking their new habitats. (See chapter 6.)

There was, however, one area where we doubted the Chinese information right away. They told us that both animals were the same age — a year and a half — when they arrived. The smaller Hsing-Hsing, they said, was just underweight because he had not eaten well shortly after he was captured. And he had been in captivity less time than the female, which would account for the shyness he demonstrated from the outset at the National Zoological Park.

On the other hand, Desmond and Ramona Morris, in their book, *Men and Pandas,* are quite explicit about the age-weight relationships of pandas. They included a chart which goes as follows:

5 ounces	0 months (i.e., at birth)
7 pounds	2 months
20 pounds	5 months
60 pounds	10 months

80 pounds	12 months
120 pounds	16 months

These figures were based upon carefully collected data from several captive pandas and we had no reason to doubt them. They indicated that Hsing-Hsing, at 74 pounds on arrival, was just about a year old while Ling-Ling, at 136, was a year and a half. And these age estimates fit with information the Chinese gave us concerning the breeding cycle of wild pandas. There are two breeding seasons each year — a primary one in the spring and a secondary one in the fall. The gestation period, they told us, was from 118 days to 168 days. From this, plus the Morris data, we determined that Ling-Ling was a year and a half old on arrival here in April 1972, having been born in the fall of 1970 from an April or May breeding. Hsing-Hsing was born in April 1971, from a fall breeding of the previous year. Not only had he spent less time in captivity — both animals had been trapped in the wild, the Chinese said — but he was also six months younger. This was enough to explain the difference in the two pandas' behavior. And indeed as we were to find out, Hsing-Hsing ran almost exactly six months behind Ling-Ling in behavior as well as size.

It is only in the matter of age that we have had any reason to doubt the Chinese information and in that case it may have been a breakdown in interpretation. Otherwise, their data has proved out so far. Pandas do, after all, come from China and the people at the Peking Zoo have had not only the greatest experience with giant pandas but the greatest successes. At the time of Ling-Ling and Hsing-Hsing's arrival here, there were several in the Peking Zoo. One of these was a nineteen-year-old male who was still vigorous and in good health, and a twenty-year-old female, Li-Li, who showed no signs of senility. This is apparently the longevity record for captive pandas; no one knows how long they live in the wild. The greatest age achieved by pandas in Western zoos has been fifteen years.

There has never been a successful breeding outside of China. Since the People's Republic was founded, however, the Chinese told us that there have been five births in the Peking Zoo, resulting in eight young, and two births in Shanghai. Of these ten infants born in captivity, they report that only two animals have survived. (We were told that pandas often give birth to multiple young, both in zoos and in the wild, but only one from such a birth has any chance of surviving in the wild: The mother holds her infant to her breast as she moves around on three legs. Thus one of twins does not survive.) Raising young pandas in captivity appears to be something of an art.

Perhaps it is for this reason, along with their universal appeal, that the giant panda was made the symbol of the World Wildlife Fund, an international organization devoted to the preservation of the earth's wildlife, especially its endangered species. Are pandas endangered? Certainly they are rare. They occur in only one place in the world, a fairly limited geographic range in the high mountainous regions of western China, primarily in the province of Szechuan. At one time they were apparently more widespread but shrank back to their present range, probably as much because of changes in

As we soon learned, the pandas are fast. Here Ling-Ling is at full stride across her outdoor paddock. (Photograph by O. H. Hertzler)

climate as from pressure from predators. No one—
except maybe the Chinese—knows how many there are
now in the wild, but it is certain that within the con-
fines of their cold habitat, bamboo forests from 5,000 to
12,000 feet, they are relatively sparse. From accounts
by the early explorers and hunters, it seems clear that
pandas do not congregate in quantity but rather leave
plenty of space between each other, leading solitary
lives for most of the year. They have few natural ene-
mies: A pack of wild dogs might possibly be capable of
taking a panda, and perhaps a leopard could as well,
though an adult panda would be a good match for any
big cat, particularly in the cramped, low tunnels of
bamboo the pandas frequent.

In fact, the greatest threat to pandas has always been
that archpredator, man. For a few decades, back in the
1920s and 1930s, a panda skin was especially presti-
gious booty for wealthy Western hunters. It may well
have been the very inaccessibility of their mountain
habitat that has saved pandas from extermination. In
any event, the People's Republic of China clamped
down on panda hunting, poaching and any other kind
of interference with these animals, and since 1949 the
giant panda has been as well protected as man can
arrange.

On the other hand, the supply of pandas in the West
took a severe drop shortly after Ling-Ling and Hsing-
Hsing arrived. By midsummer, Chi-Chi died in London,
leaving our two pandas as the only ones in the Free
World, though their very presence here symbolized the
breakdown of such Cold War distinctions. With An-An's

death in Moscow on October 15, ours were for the moment the only ones outside of the Orient (where eighteen remained in Chinese zoos and three in North Korea). So the staff of the National Zoo, especially the four keepers and I, felt a particularly heavy responsibility for the well-being of our two fragile but explosive clowns.

Hsing-Hsing. (Photograph by Larry Collins)

3

Well-being

Heaven is a piece of honey bread.

— DAVE BRYAN

Think, for a moment, about bamboo. If you have never seen a fresh piece of bamboo, you probably have seen the yellowish-tan, shiny segmented sticks of bamboo that are often rolled up in carpets or seen lying around uselessly in garages. They are very hard, very splintery — the sort of object that immediately suggests to a small boy a pole for pole vaulting. But even a small boy would never think about eating such a thing.

The real difference between an old yellow bamboo pole and the fresh stalks that are brought daily and dumped outside the Panda House for Ling-Ling and Hsing-Hsing is that fresh stalks have leaves and are green, not yellow. But they are just about as hard and, if anything, they are springier. Now then, having thought about it, how would you eat bamboo? You would eat the leaves, not the stalk. A panda will eat both, but it will eat the leaves first, given the chance.

How to eat bamboo

From the outset both Ling-Ling and Hsing-Hsing were very interested in the bamboo planted in pots in their enclosures. For Hsing-Hsing, the bamboo pots seemed like something of a refuge. We often found him sitting shyly in a pot, looking demurely out from behind the narrow green leaves, eating some of the greenery, of course, but also just sitting there. Ling-Ling, on the other hand always has used her bamboo as an object for exercise as well as food, tearing up the stalks and strewing them about her enclosure with her usual mixture of playfulness and pique. (Hsing-Hsing learned to do this too as he grew older.) But they both eat it as well, stalks and all, and their ability to do so takes a little explaining.

The best explanation is that of Desmond Morris who wrote: "The whole head of the giant panda has become modified as a crunching machine." Large muscles connect a broad, blunt-toothed jaw to a vast heavy skull. (Hsing-Hsing seems to have an especially big head, in fact.) It is an extraordinarily efficient crunching machine, capable of biting through one-and-a-half-inch-thick bamboo stalks and, as we learned, putting tooth holes in unbitable toys. Also, we knew, it is easily capable of snapping off a human wristbone.

Once bitten off, a piece of bamboo would seem a highly indigestible item, calling for an extraordinary stomach. The giant panda's stomach, as well as that of the bamboo-eating lesser panda, *is* extraordinary, but oddly enough it is what one would imagine to be extraordinarily unsuited to eating bamboo. The intestines of these animals are uniquely short, providing little room (and time) for digesting. And, it turns out, pandas get little nourishment from a piece of bamboo. To make up for this, they eat a great deal of it in the wild, wandering casually around in the bamboo stands of their mountainous habitat, browsing during almost

How to eat bamboo: first you select the right stalk as Ling-Ling is doing here. (Photograph by Smithsonian Institution)

How to eat bamboo: then you hold it in your paw and pull it down, as Ling-Ling demonstrates. (Photograph by Smithsonian Institution)

How to eat bamboo: being careful not to let the stalk spring back up, Ling-Ling samples the leaves. (Photograph by Smithsonian Institution)

all their waking hours, and leaving a telltale trail of droppings behind that were as useful to panda hunters of old as were the little white stones to Hansel and Gretel. In addition, wild pandas also eat other vegetable matter including such gentle fodder as crocuses, irises and gentians.

For Ling-Ling and Hsing-Hsing, the keepers harvest some twenty pounds of fresh, cut bamboo daily — nowhere near enough to sustain them if that were all they ate (more about that later). But cut bamboo is one thing. To see Ling-Ling and Hsing-Hsing take on a twenty-foot bamboo stalk growing from a two-hundred-pound pot or from the ground of their outdoor enclosures is to understand a little bit of how a giant panda operates in the wild, and also to get a notion of why they seem so appealingly intelligent.

On many occasions, I have watched transfixed as Ling-Ling approached a living stalk of bamboo in her outdoor enclosure. She stands up on her hind legs and, reaching upward, takes a grip high on the stalk with her forepaws. With a firm grasp on it, she slowly falls over backward, pulling the stalk down with her until it looks something like a primitive catapult. Of course, it would act like a catapult too if she did not roll over on all fours and loop one hind leg over it so that it will not snap upright. Then she inches along the stalk toward the leaves and, often reclining on her side or back, munches until she is satisfied. As she dines, she holds the spring-loaded stalk with one forepaw while she manipulates it with the other. Once satisfied, she rolls away and the bamboo stalk snaps up, to be finished later. Hsing-Hsing follows the same procedure.

It is unlikely that a cat or dog or most other animals could accomplish such a feat even if the idea crossed their minds to try it, and one reason lies in the panda's grip. They use their forepaws much like hands and this

How to eat bamboo: Another style, shown by Ling-Ling, is simply to get on top of it. (Photograph by Larry Collins)

How to eat bamboo: The ultimate reward is something thick to gnaw on and, in this part of bamboo-eating, it is useful to have a big head like Hsing-Hsing's. (Photograph by Smithsonian Institution)

is possible because of something called the *radial sesamoid* bone, an elongated wristbone on each front paw, covered with a tough horny pad of skin. (See page 126.) It lies opposite the panda's five claws, just about where you would expect a thumb to be and it acts very much like a thumb, the animal being able to close its first two "fingers" against it in a grasping motion. With the exception of the lesser panda, which has a relatively far less developed sesamoid bone, there is nothing like this "thumb" or "sixth claw" to be found anywhere in the animal kingdom. The sesamoid bone and pad can move, along with the five claws, to create an extremely strong grip, perfect for clutching a stalk of bamboo or nearly anything else a panda might come across. Not only is it a power grip but it can work with considerable precision. This ability to hold onto things is one quality which, I think, gives visitors the strong impression that there is something human about pandas. Consider the eating of an apple, a frequent snack the two pandas receive. The apple is bitten in half and each half is held in a forepaw. Then, sitting spraddle-legged, leaning its back against the log platform or a wall, the panda sits comfortably looking around the enclosure eating one half and then the other.

Some anthropologists say that there was a feedback loop in the evolution of the human species wherein the brain grew large and clever only as the thumb grew to be opposable to the fingers, permitting a precision grip. Dexterity fed cleverness and cleverness permitted more dextrous and inventive uses of the hand. It is not very scientific but it is a pleasant, romantic, and unavoidable notion one gets watching Ling-Ling or Hsing-

Hsing holding an apple that one day, given several thousand or million years, a group of large furry, black and white creatures might set out to build a suspension bridge.

Bread and honey and other delicacies

It pays to keep an eye on the undemonstrative member of a group. When the group consists of two, it is also not hard to do, but visitors are inclined to notice what the flamboyant female, Ling-Ling, does and sometimes miss some subtleties of panda behavior exhibited by the conservative Hsing-Hsing.

Take, for example, honey bread.

Pandas may have evolved as bamboo-eaters, but a piece of bread with honey on it is a singular delicacy for these animals. The Chinese mentioned this and all of us at the Panda House soon learned its value. When it was time, for instance, to clean up Ling-Ling's cage, to put in new bamboo and replace the dirt in her bamboo pots, it was very important that Ling-Ling be elsewhere — preferably in her den with the door shut. This could best be accomplished by throwing a piece of honey bread into her den and, when she went for it, closing the door behind her. Not until she had stuffed this exquisite morsel in her mouth and swallowed it would she realize she had been had and throw herself with a resounding thump against the door. (At least, it used to work that way. On several notable occasions, described later, this strategem did not work so smoothly.)

Such tricks invariably worked on Hsing-Hsing but, characteristically, he had his own way of dealing with a piece of honey bread and it has never varied since his arrival. A typical incident illustrates not only his particular style but the esteem in which he regards this heavenly delicacy.

Dave Bryan and I returned from lunch one crisp sunny day in January and thought it a good idea to give the pandas a snack. Sliding the door open between the male's den and the keeper's area just far enough so that his head would not fit through, I held out a carrot.

"Hey, Hsing, come on over here."

He raised his head, looked, and lumbered over to us. Poking his nose through the opening, he snuffled at the carrot, and decided it was time instead for a back rub. He lowered his head between his forepaws, resting his broad forehead on the floor, and thrust his shoulders into the opening. I scratched him with the carrot for a moment and said:

"Hey! Hsing! Here's a carrot!"

He raised his head, spotted the carrot, and swiftly dropped his head to the floor again, shifting his weight so that a new spot on his shoulder blades was presented for scratching. (We believe that Hsing-Hsing would be quite content to spend the remainder of his years in some air-conditioned out-of-the-way massage parlor, having his back scratched.) While this ritual continued, Dave left and came back shortly with a piece of white bread smeared with honey. He flipped it through the open door, over Hsing-Hsing's shoulders, onto the cement floor. The panda looked up at us and our carrot, looked down at the floor, backed up deftly, picked up the bread with one forepaw and took a delicate bite. Then, lips smacking, he turned the bread a few degrees in his paw and took another fastidious bite. And in the manner of some small children who save the best till last, he proceeded—as always—to eat all the crust off his bread before stuffing the honey-covered center into his jaws. (As the year progressed, some of the glow left honey bread and we had begun using carrots as the chief bribe for Ling-Ling.)

There is another apparent delicacy for the pandas, but in their first year Hsing-Hsing was the only one who may have enjoyed it so far as we know, though I would have bet on Ling-Ling. On the day Mrs. Nixon welcomed the pandas, shortly after all the dignitaries had left the Panda House, a few stragglers noted that while Ling-Ling was lying on her back on her log platform, a mouse was peering out from a crack between the logs just a few feet below her. Ultimately she noticed this tiny cagemate and lay on her chaise longue peering over the edge intently at it until it disappeared under the logs. She may have caught it later, unbeknownst to us, but Hsing-Hsing has been less secretive in such matters. There is a loose-leaf notebook that is kept in the kitchen adjoining the pandas' enclosures. It serves as a log of important events and amid its more elaborate descriptions of feeding, play, and other activities, it bears the following entries:

11-1-72   Hsing killed a mouse in his cage last night.
Tex Rowe

11-17-72   Hsing killed a mouse.

Dave Bryan

It should be a surprise to no one that pandas, descended from the carnivores and considered carnivores themselves, though they rely mostly on bamboo in the wild, would hunt a mouse. In nature they are also known to take and eat small mammals such as mice and voles as well as birds. (Nor should it be much of a surprise that, various health and security precautions notwithstanding, zoo animals often share their enclosures with mice. Most people do as well.)

Staples, weight gains, and house calls

Honey bread and carrots are special fillips to the pandas' diets. Even bamboo supplies only a part of their daily fare. Grass is sometimes an unplanned snack: It was not long after the pandas were allowed to go into their outside enclosures that Ling-Ling had dug up welcome-mat-sized pieces of turf and was grazing on the divots. But all of this alone would not sustain these two eager eaters. The staple of their diets has been the same since their first meal here—rice gruel with multivitamin and mineral additives, apples and carrots. To that we have added sweet potatoes (boiled), "Milk-bone" dog biscuits (for *large* dogs), and bread and honey, and we have increased the quantities steadily. (Detailed menus are to be found in Appendix A.)

The pandas receive a main feeding at 9:30 A.M. and another main feeding at 4 P.M. They also receive a noontime snack of apples and carrots. We prefer to have some of each meal left behind; then we know the animals have eaten their fill. They almost always leave some. The results of all this trencherwork are readily apparent in the rapid weight gains the animals made in their first year in Washington. Each month the animals are coaxed onto the scale. Weighing them involves shutting each one in its den, rolling platform-type scales into its inside enclosure, and placing them flush against the pandaproof glass. The wheels on the scales are locked and the weighing mechanism unlocked. The den door is then opened and the animal is given access to its enclosure. Being curious beasts by nature, they carefully investigate anything new in their enclosures and this quickly leads them to climb up on the weighing platforms to have a look. Their weights are recorded by the keeper looking at the face of the scale through the pandaproof glass. Once in a while a honey-bread bribe is used to help speed things up. Since the animals are weighed only once a month, the novelty of the scales doesn't wear off and the weighing process usually only takes fifteen minutes for both animals. This ritual was once preceded by a pool among the keepers and me, in which we guessed what Hsing-Hsing's weight would be.

Bribed by a piece of honey bread, Ling-Ling sits on the scales, unaware that she has been so helpful. (Photograph by Col. Steve Slaughter)

The table below shows the weights on arrival and, beginning in September when we obtained the proper scales for weighing the animals out of their crates, the dramatic gains they made, especially the male.

	Hsing-Hsing	Ling-Ling
April 16, 1972	74	136
September 1972	128°	170
October 1972	137	175
November 1972	146	179
December 1972	158	186
January 1973	172	200
February 1973	182	213
March 1973	203	224

Throughout the fall and winter Hsing-Hsing gained an average of about 10 pounds a month — you could almost see him grow. On October 27, when Hsing-Hsing weighed in at 137 pounds, Tex Rowe wrote in the log: "It is interesting to me to note that, from weights at time of arrival, we figured him to be six months younger than the female. Now approximately six months later his weight is nearly identical to her weight at that time." Ultimately, when adult, they will reach 300 pounds and be six feet from stem to stern.

Just as a good appetite is a sign of health, any loss of appetite or other aberration in the pandas' regular habits is a sign of immediate concern which can set off an

° Curley Harper won the pool, guessing the exact weight. Dave Bryan was next closest with 125, Tex Rowe at 124. I was way off: 135.

"alarm" that brings the zoo staff running. And on a few occasions there have been such aberrations.

One morning in the fall of 1972 Hsing-Hsing showed a reluctance to eat at his regular feeding time. Dr. Mitchell Bush, the zoo's clinical veterinarian was called and arrived minutes later, by which time the panda had begun to eat slowly, finishing in about an hour. We thought it might be because he had been outside that morning, which often delays his appetite. But the next morning he showed the same reluctance and he had not been outdoors. Yet the enclosure showed signs of more than usual nocturnal activity—that is, it was a mess— so perhaps he was merely tired from a big night. But by eleven o'clock he still had not eaten, so again, Dr. Bush was summoned. And, to everyone's relief, once again Hsing-Hsing began eating at about eleven-thirty.

Such incidents seem relatively mild as a cause for alarm, but as far as the pandas are concerned, we do not worry about crying wolf. It is better to have Dr. Bush on hand, even if it turns out to be just a matter of a panda deciding to have a late breakfast. (The same of course applies to the rest of our zoo animals.) Another time it *was* serious.

On July 22, 1972, a hot muggy Saturday when Tex Rowe and Curley Harper were on duty, Tex scratched the following hastily into the log:

22 July—Female was sleeping in den this A.M. which is unusual. After cleaning cages, we were in kitchen preparing food when officer on duty (Bennett) reported to us that Ling had vomited and ate it back. Curley Harper observed a repeat of this minutes later. Animal breathing hard, ap-

pears uncomfortable, coughed three times in succession. Lots of "lip-licking." Very inactive, appears "beat." Cage temperature 72°.

Called Dr. Bush—expected at hospital soon. Left call-back message.

Called L. Collins—operator reported number out of service. [The switchboard had dialed the wrong number.]

Called Dr. Garner—no answer.

Called Dr. Reed—coming in.

Officer Bennett cleared and closed building at our request at approximately 9:30 A.M. Held off feeding till Dr. Bush arrived, followed soon by Dr. Reed.

Dr. Bush recommended light feeding of small amount of rice formula plus some sliced carrots for Ling-Ling. Ate only a small amount of rice and rested in doorway, still breathing hard. Added a few bamboo leaves.

11:30—Now seems to be resting comfortably, though not sleeping and not in usual place or position. Still no more food consumption.

11:45—Got up and ate remainder of food. In meantime water tub was put in cage on Dr. Reed's order.

12:00—Got in her tub for short bath, out and batted ball around a bit, back in tub, then back to playing ball, then to her usual tub in the corner for a dust bath, and a bit more play around the cage to 12:20. Acting "normal."

By two o'clock that day we had put a 300-pound cake of ice in both enclosures: clearly it had been too warm in the building. The male broke off a piece and juggled it on his feet, then grasping it in his forepaws rubbed it all over his stomach; the female sat on hers, slid on it, then broke off a piece and ate it. A large, mobile air conditioner was hastily furnished by Andrews Air Force

Base to supplement the main unit and Ling-Ling, on two-thirds rations (plus extra salt), ate very well that afternoon. By the next afternoon, Dr. Bush put his patient back on full ration and the incident was over.

Dr. Bush probably makes as many house calls as all the doctors in the District of Columbia put together.

More medical matters

Soon after his arrival, we noticed roundworms in Hsing-Hsing's droppings — no surprise since the Chinese had told us that roundworms are a common parasite problem with giant pandas. And we wormed him just the way you (or the vet) would worm your dog. We administered piperazine adipate in a dosage of one grain per pound of body weight, and the situation cleared up quickly and satisfactorily. Subsequently we made periodic parasitological checks of both pandas' stools and they always proved negative. The nature of a captive animal's feces can be an important indication of its well-being in general and so, as with virtually every aspect of the pandas' lives, we pay close attention here as well. We had been advised not to get alarmed if the pandas' stools were loose and yellow-to-orange since this is normal for captive pandas. However, for the most part, Hsing-Hsing's and Ling-Ling's droppings were ovoid, firm, and very fibrous — identical to the droppings described for free-living pandas. We suspect this is because of their heavy diet of bamboo:

some 10–12 pounds a day. Not only is this a sign of health on the part of the pandas, but it is more pleasant for the keepers. The pandas' enclosures are remarkably odor free.

Another primary medical concern we had was to assure that both pandas were immunized against canine and feline distemper, a killer of many unprotected young carnivores. In the earliest days, before they received shots, the pandas were sealed off as much as possible from contact with people. Only the keepers, when they had to clean the enclosures and feed the animals, and the gardeners, when they had to transplant bamboo, were allowed inside. I even excluded myself from entering since my presence inside was not absolutely essential. And those who did go in went through procedures something like researchers in a germ-free laboratory: They had to put on freshly autoclaved coveralls and surgical boots and had to walk through a foot bath on the way in. On June 9, both pandas received their first series of distemper shots, an inactivated vaccine that also protects them against canine hepatitis and leptospirosis. Within a month they had received two more inoculations and six months later, in January, booster shots.

Naturally you don't walk up and stick a needle in a giant panda, particularly the Ling-Ling variety of giant panda. They had to be restrained and to do so we took advantage of their considerable curiosity. Each panda's access to its outdoor paddock is gained by passing through an expanded metal, panda-sized cage attached to the building at the back door of the animal's den.

While keeper Tex Rowe holds a carrot as a reward, Dr. Mitchell Bush gives Ling-Ling a shot while she is restrained in her squeeze cage. Mike Johnson is at left. (Photograph by *National Geographic*)

When we want to restrain one of them, we drop a clear plexiglass door in the front end of the cage and then open the den door (which also serves as the back door of the cage). Believing that it has a chance to go outside, the panda proceeds into the cage and we close the den door behind it. One side of the cage has double sides. The inner second side is hinged and we close it snugly, on the panda, rendering it quite immobile whenever necessary. The whole apparatus is called a squeeze cage. Squeezing is rarely necessary, in fact, since both pandas enjoy having their backs scratched and readily press themselves against the side of the cage asking for this treat. Dr. Bush usually scratches with one hand and injects with the other and most of the time the pandas don't seem to know they have been injected. Another fail-safe distraction is a piece of honey bread or a carrot. Not only are the shots decidedly untraumatic; the pandas also don't seem to mind at all being restrained in the familiar surroundings of their squeeze cages. They exhibit no stress or discomfort at such times and, when the plexiglass is gone and the den door open, neither shows any hesitancy about lumbering through to the outdoors, even immediately after being confined.

By the end of their first year in Washington, the pandas had grown rapidly. They spent increasing amounts of time in vigorous play. All this burned up fuel and their diets were increased accordingly. (Eventually the quantity of food will stabilize and we will all become weight watchers: adult captive pandas tend to obesity.) All in all, they showed all the signs of healthy animals, from clinical tests to those more subtle, less definable but equally important indications of well-being — much the same kinds of things that mothers look for in their children. Only in this case the mothers happen to be four men.

The original panda unit: Standing from left to right, Tex Rowe, Curley Harper, Mike Johnson, Dave Bryan. Kneeling is Larry Collins. (Photograph by Larry Collins)

4

Cool Dudes

I don't know how many times I've been told,
"You can't bring *that* in this house."

—TEX ROWE

This chapter is about four animal keepers, the original four members of an elite, low-down, professional group whose job is to see that two pandas stay healthy. They are craftsmen in a sense, something like artists. As Curley Harper says, talking about a previous assignment, "I'd go in the Monkey House in the morning and I could tell if something was wrong from the smell. Right away I'd say, 'Someone in here ain't together today. I don't know which one of you it is, but I'll find out.'"

All four keepers are as different as you could ask. They come from different backgrounds, from various parts of the country, and they reached the Panda House by various routes. As befits the keepers of pandas, two are black and two are white. They vary in age, experience, marital status and in most personal preferences. But first and foremost, they are animal men and they quickly became a unit in the truest sense. One night I asked each one when he got interested in animals: it was a long night.

There is no particular order but we might as well start with Tex Rowe since he got started with animals first.

Tex Rowe

"Let's see, it was fifty-one years, six months and two days ago. Does that make it June 21, 1921? Because I was born interested in animals."

Tex wears a whitish-blond, spade-shaped beard with a curling handlebar mustache, and he owns a pair of finely tooled cowboy boots with silver plates on the toes and heels. He must have been in a thousand towns, and he can remember just about every fence post in between. When he tells you where he has been, it sounds like the schedules of the old railroads that tied the West to the East in those days. Tex was a traveling man and he has a thousand yarns.

When he was young, he walked several miles to school every day and once, at age seven, he stopped off on the way home and asked a farmer for a job. "Don't want no pay," he explained, "I just want a job." So he fed the farmer's horses and eventually his hogs, too, on the way home from school every day.

"It must have been April — I was just under thirteen — when I ran to the circus. Not away. *To* the circus." He became a pony punk at first. All youngsters, including baby elephants, are called "punks" in the circus. He took care of the horses all summer and then went back to school. "I had a hell of a time getting through school," he says, "because every April when the paper went up (meaning the circus posters), off I'd go." His father could always find him when he disappeared by reading the schedule of the circus and waiting in the next town.

Once he had made it through school, Tex went on the road all year around. If you ask him what he did in the circus, he will stop for a moment and say, "It would be quicker if I tell you what I didn't do." He handled ponies, dogs, big cats, primates. He was a barker: "A feller showed me how to sell a crowd an empty tent — twice in one night." In 1940, he made a big mistake. Instead of going south with the show, he stopped off for the winter in Pennsylvania. Before long his money was gone and, "to keep warm," he joined the horse cavalry at Fort Bliss, Texas. Technological progress (and Tex's luck) being what it was, he wound up in aircraft gunnery in Denver, Colorado, where it was 30 below zero. After serving in the South Pacific where at least it was warmer, he was mustered out in 1945 and made his way to San Francisco by means of his thumb. There a man named Brooklyn Blackie taught him the "tattoo trade." (Tex is now tattooed from his ankles to his neck. The names of most of the carnivals he has been in are inscribed on his right leg. "There wasn't room for them all.")

From San Francisco he went back on the road with the circus. Every so often he would stop off somewhere for the winter: "Wintertimes you do pretty near everything." Once he stayed for nearly two years in San Antonio, Texas. Another winter layover turned into two and a half years in Tennessee. But each time he would eventually pick up and move on, until 1959 when he realized he was "absolutely tired from running around." He went home to San Antonio and stayed in the back of a secondhand bookstore and from there he applied by mail for a job at the National Zoological Park and with an animal dealer in Cleveland and one in New York. To get closer, or perhaps because motion was by now a habit, he went to Pittsburgh where, while waiting for a reply, he opened up a tattoo joint for a while and survived yet another winter by gambling. "Man who comes in and says 'Well, I've got five dollars to lose tonight' is telling me that I've got five dollars to *win*. Add up all the threes and fives that these jokers have to lose and you're all right for a winter."

He applied again to the National Zoological Park, then went back on the road. He did a stint as manager of a "junky zoo" in the Pocono Mountains, and yet another as a bartender. Having bought himself a pony named Smokey, he acquired a chimpanzee as well, and before long found himself near Scranton and helping a man build a zoo which subsequently had to move to Altoona. By this time it was 1966 and he called the National Zoo on the telephone. Before long he was working in the Reptile House, where all new keepers began in those days. Later he was transferred to the Small Mammals House. Still the owner of some animals in a small zoo in Ligonier, Pennsylvania, he happened to be away visiting them when the list was passed around for volunteers for the Panda Unit. But we found him anyway.

Dave Bryan

Dave Bryan is a big man with large hands. He looks as if he might have been an athlete. He is regularly kidded by the rest of us as being the man who started to spell his name wrong on the "What's My Line?" blackboard. And he quickly points out that it was a bad week up in New York. "The producer told me that the week before a contestant walked in from behind the curtain and the man said, 'Will the next challenger sign in, please?' She started to write, looked out at that audience, and just fell right over in a dead faint.

That producer was having an awful week." Apparently Dave's attraction to animals is written all over him. The panel guessed his line after five questions.

Dave started out in Maryland. He had a cat named Mitten, later a dog as well, and "for some strange reason" got interested in birds at the age of twelve. First it was homing pigeons. "I built myself some kind of jive coop, but it didn't work out too well. The cat kept getting the pigeons." His father, who was a preacher, rendered the coop catproof, and Dave kept buying pigeons, entering them in pigeon races in which the birds are taken as far as 500 miles from home and released. Once he won a $75 race.

Before long he got interested in chickens, too, finding it fascinating to watch them. He built another coop and bought chickens. "My father said, 'What next?'" Easter was next and a lady in the neighborhood received two ducks which she didn't know what to do with. Dave took them. "My father said, 'What next?'" Rabbits and squirrels were next and eventually winter came. It was, Dave thought, too cold for the young chicks, so he brought them into his room to overwinter in the warmth. That was too much for the patient preacher and the chickens returned to the coop.

When he reached high school, girls and basketball replaced animals as the focus of interest, but one summer he joined a neighborhood youth corps program ("one of those things they had to get hoodlums off the streets") and became one of a hundred youths who were told they would be working at the Smithsonian Institution as guides. Of the hundred, ten were to be assigned to the National Zoological Park. "Everybody was just waiting around to be assigned to one place or another but I didn't see no point in going to a museum. So I went up to the man and said I'd like the zoo. He must have been surprised at having a volunteer so that's where I went."

For two summers he worked in the Large Mammal Division and then graduation from high school left him "with this urge to make some money." He got a temporary, one-year appointment to the Large Mammal Division as an animal keeper and when it was over, secured another one-year appointment. At this time he received his "greetings" from another branch of government and quickly enlisted in the Navy. By the end of this hitch he was in Andros Island in the Bahamas, an expert at retrieving and disarming torpedoes. Life was good: "You got three hots and a cot, and those girls down there were beautiful. One day in Nassau I fell in love twenty-six times in thirty minutes just standing on a street corner."

The Navy asked him to stay on and work in a special torpedo unit. "But I was getting tired of being out riding the seas every time I turned around. You know. I was getting seasick." And, he realized, he was homesick. So he returned to Maryland and picked up where he had left off as a keeper in Large Mammals. He was assigned to the Delicate Hoof Stock House Number One, taking care of the white rhinos, kangaroos, and bongos. So when they were evacuated to make room for Ling-Ling and Hsing-Hsing, Dave didn't have to move an inch.

Curley Harper

When you first see Curley Harper, you think of a musician, not an animal keeper. And, among many other things, Curley was a musician. He carries with him a certain air of caution, of wisdom gained from a life that hasn't been easy. He is inclined to look at things from a slightly different angle than most people.

One night Tex was explaining how to train dogs (he was a dog trainer, too) and told how he had once had some eleven dogs living with him. They weren't, for obvious reasons, allowed on the bed and would never go there even when Tex was gone — except for one that he just couldn't train properly. Whenever Tex left, this one dog would immediately get on the bed and dig it up. Sitting back in a chair, his eyes closed, Curley listened and said with a smile, "You don't mean to say they were all smart except the one dog, do you? I'd say that one dog was the smart one. Did just what he wanted whenever he could." Curley has his own way of looking at things through an animal's eyes.

He was born in an area called The Flats in Youngstown, Ohio, and seemed always to be interested in animals. "I used to sit so long in the cold out in the woods watching wild animals that my feet would turn orange." Like Dave Bryan he kept chickens, including one that rode with him on his bike. After high school and two years at Federal City College he worked in a laundry, and then in an auto plant—"You know, sweepin' the floors and that kind of stuff till I was fired. So I was enjoying unemployment and then I met a guy named Foley who got me a job in a steel mill." He worked there seven years, was laid off, and again enjoyed eighteen months of unemployment. He worked a while in a body shop and then played the drums in a small band.

A friend persuaded him to come to Washington. "I arrived in D.C. with fourteen dollars in a greasy bag." The friend got him a job watching weasels and monkeys in a private biological laboratory. From there, he went to the National Institutes of Health and became a laboratory technician, but it grew boring. "It was like listening to a tape. Same thing, over and over." A friend of his, formerly an employee of the National Zoological Park but at this time engaged in bonding ex-convicts, helped him to get a job at the zoo.

"I went to reptiles, to the commissary, the lion house, the bird house, small mammals, large mammals, monkeys—I got rotated. That was the policy then, but also I was supposed to be hard to get along with. Like I say to my kids, 'Oh, what ugly children my momma had, but no dumb ones!' " (Curley has five children.)

"The Panda House. That's the place for me to be. One day one of the guys came from Administration over to the Panda House. Dave and Mike and I were on duty and the guy said, 'Who's in charge?' I told him there wasn't anyone in charge. 'There's got to be someone in charge,' he said, 'Who's in charge?'

"And I said, 'Ain't nobody in charge here now. We're all just taking care of the pandas, man.'"

Mike Johnson

Once, when Mike Johnson compared the dangers of dealing with Ling-Ling to those of handling crocodiles or wrestling bears, I challenged him. He had worked in the Reptile House and had manhandled crocs, but, I said, "Come on, man, what do you know about wrestling bears?"

"I got in the ring with a bear once," he said. "I was in high school and I'd just taken up wrestling and there was this show—you know, a kind of trade show. One of the events was bear wrestling. You got fifty bucks if you could stay in the ring with this bear they had there. He was muzzled.

"I watched one dude go in there and try out his karate. You know, a big deal. He came up and hit the bear and of course you don't go around hitting bears because it makes them mad. So the bear hit the dude back and knocked him right out of the ring.

"I was next and I figured I could probably get him with some of those cool wrestling holds I'd learned. And I did get a reverse on him, but then he sat on me and it was all over — *all* over."

At this time, Mike was in his wrestling and football stage, one of the few, short times when animals were not much on his mind. He had grown up in Ohio and had hunted with his father and his father's spaniels, learning about the habits of wild game as he learned to work the dogs. He collected snakes, kept turtles in cages, and raised six raccoons. Until high school athletics temporarily weaned him away, he wanted to be a veterinarian.

Before his senior year, his family moved to Maryland, and a new friend, whose sport was archery, took him to the Patuxent River. "I saw a big black rat snake in the woods there and had this old urge — so I captured it and took it home and was back into animals." During his last year in high school he kept a tankful of tropical fish and, after graduation, went back to Patuxent and let the rat snake go free. A year later he had flunked out of Frostberg State College in Maryland, and, instead of taking a more lucrative job in construction, went to work in a tropical fish store and at the same time applied for a job at the National Zoological Park. In 1968, he was hired at the zoo and, though he had been asked to be manager of the fish store, went to work (you guessed it) in the Reptile House.

But of course, reptiles and amphibians were just what Mike wanted. He worked with lizards and snakes and in the aquarium (where they kept turtles and amphibians). "Then I graduated to the hot stuff—the adders and cobras. I got *super*interested in animals then. Working with live animals is nothing like any zoology course. You get attuned to their behavior."

He was detailed to the Bird Division for thirty days and developed an interest in birds of prey. He still goes out on occasional assignments to catch wild ones for zoos and, being something of a collector himself, keeps six (!) screech owls in his apartment. After his stint in the Bird Division, Mike returned happily to reptiles, but snakes, he had decided, "aren't with it." Mike rhapsodizes over lizards and turtles. "Lizards have their territories and you can go in the cage and *see* the communication going on. Lizards and turtles—they know what's happening."

While on a trip to Europe and Russia, Mike had seen An-An, the giant panda in Moscow, so when the call came for volunteers for the panda unit, he decided to try mammals. "It was kind of an ego trip; but I never thought I'd be picked." But of course he was.

That, then, is the original panda unit—except for me. My route to the Panda House was perfectly straightforward. I was studying to be a dentist and, while taking a required zoology course, I wound up with a pet brown bat that would eat mealworms out of my hand. So naturally I went on to study Australian marsupials: They called me Captain Kangaroo at the zoo until the pandas came.

The original four panda keepers are now three. Mike Johnson was called back to the Reptile House in the fall of 1972. He was promoted to biological technician and began work on a difficult project to breed captive leatherback turtles, huge seagoing turtles which are on the list of endangered species. The hope is that, if they can be induced to breed in captivity, it may be possible to replenish the dwindling natural populations. Also he takes on assignments working with birds of prey.

I asked Mike if he missed being a keeper. "It's great being a technician," he said, "and it's a great chance to learn and to move up. Someday I'd like to be a curator of a reptile house. But being a keeper is something else. An animal keeper is a real professional, too. Maybe I'm a little romantic, but that's the way I feel about it. When I was a little kid in Toledo, I spent a lot of time at the zoo with my grandparents. I was around the zoo so much that I got to go behind the scenes a lot. I thought then — and I still do — that the keepers were the greatest. They were cool dudes."

Ling-Ling. (Photograph by Stan Wayman)

5

Play

Voilà! The Pandaproof Toy
— headline in the Washington *Post*

June 1, 1972 was supposed to be one of the most historic days in the pandas' young lives — a double-header, in fact. They were to be given their first opportunity to go outdoors, and, once there, they would see each other for the first time. It was a day full of expectation — on our parts; the pandas, of course, had no idea what was in store. And, of course, it did not work out as we had planned.

First sight

On the other side of the doors leading out from the pandas' enclosures are the squeeze cages I described before. Beyond these squeeze cages are alleyways which lead into the two adjacent 35-by-60-foot paddocks. The paddock walls are some seven feet high and made of wood, except for the wall that separates the two paddocks. This is made of strong wire-mesh fence about three feet high, topped by wooden planks some four feet high. These are temporary paddocks, to be expanded later into an area of about a half acre, and they had been planted with grass and bamboo.

Early in the morning of June 1, we opened the doors into and out of the squeeze cages, making a free passageway to the outdoor paddocks. Typically, given an opportunity to try something new, Ling-Ling immediately headed for the outdoors. She sniffed around the alleyway for a few moments and proceeded into the pen, making a complete circuit along the walls. Just as typically, Hsing-Hsing was more cautious. After several minutes, he ventured through his squeeze cage and hung around the alleyway. Then, having marked one of the paddock doors with scent, he went back inside. Eventually he made it all the way out to the paddock, but not at a time when Ling-Ling was outside too, so the day passed without the pandas becoming acquainted.

For a period of about two hours almost every day afterward when it was not too hot, the pandas were free to go in and out at will and, to our utter frustration, over two weeks passed before they happened to be outdoors at the same time. In the interval, Ling-Ling quickly made herself at home, tearing up the grass and tearing down the bamboo as fast as we could plant it. And after nine days Hsing-Hsing also felt at home in the outdoors, contentedly munching his bamboo shoots and for the most part relaxing in the grass. Our impatience grew with each day.

Early on June 16, Hsing-Hsing ambled outside and approached the wire fence. The female was standing on the other side, only a few feet away. Hsing-Hsing slapped at the fence and bleated and Ling-Ling did a complete somersault, followed by a series of sideways cartwheels. A few moments later they were nose-to-nose at the fence, bleating at each other. Then they stood on their heads. Various acrobatics ensued on both sides of the wire mesh and ultimately Ling-Ling tried to climb the fence. The first meeting had been worth waiting for.

As the summer progressed, both animals grew more accustomed to the outdoors and to each other. It seemed as if they looked forward to meeting at the fence. For example, one day we watched Hsing-Hsing emerge from the alleyway and immediately begin rolling down the slight slope along the wire fence in the classic manner of children rolling down hills. After two complete rolls he stopped, looked up and, seeing that Ling-Ling was not on the other side of the fence, gave up and walked off to chew on his bamboo. Meetings at the fence were frequent, however, and almost invariably accompanied by false charges, bleating, somersaults, foot races, and synchronized rolling. And heavy breathing. Hsing-Hsing in particular would often exert himself to the extent that we feared the heat and exercise would be too much for him. On such occasions, we would lure him back into his air-conditioned enclosure to calm down.

Indeed the heavy, muggy summers, for which Washington is notorious, posed something of a problem and there were many days during the summer when we could not let the pandas outdoors at all. They are, of course, cold-weather animals and anything over 70° is not only uncomfortable for them but unhealthy. Someone suggested that we give them a swimming pool; the Chinese, however, had told us that pandas did not like going in the water. Nonetheless, on the assumption that no panda had ever before spent a summer in Washington, we decided it was worth a try. Late in June we installed in each paddock a large wooden tub filled with water. When Ling-Ling noticed hers, her first reaction was to carefully investigate it. She approached the tub from downwind, a behavioral trait we had noticed in Hsing-Hsing as well when he is confronted with an unfamiliar object. Within a few minutes she had climbed in and taken up a now familiar pose, sitting relaxed in

Ling-Ling, in a rare cautious moment, listens in her new water tub for . . . submarines? (Photograph by *National Geographic*)

the water tub like a movie actress in a sunken bath. Hsing-Hsing's reaction was similar—only, being true to character, he took longer.

All of this activity is amusing; it has also been fairly carefully analyzed.

The four most common forms of panda play, it was discovered by Dr. Devra Kleiman, our Reproduction Zoologist, are somersaulting, headstands, lateral rolls, and head- and body-shaking. And in these, as in most things, each of the pandas has its own characteristic preferences. They both shake and roll with about the same frequency; of the four play patterns, Ling-Ling uses the roll about 40 per cent of the time, shaking about 15 per cent. For Hsing-Hsing it is 35 per cent and a little over 10 per cent respectively. It is in the business of somersaulting and headstands that they differ markedly. When Ling-Ling puts her head down to the ground, you can be pretty sure she will follow through with a somersault; of the four play patterns, somersaults are used 45 per cent of the time and practically no headstands are executed. On the other hand, almost half the times that Hsing-Hsing puts his head down on the ground to start a somersault, he gets no further than a headstand. In fact, about one-fourth of his play patterns involve standing on his big head.

The great escape attempt

In the alleyway between Ling-Ling's indoor and outdoor enclosures, a stone wall rises up to the parapet

Ling-Ling takes to water with a flourish. (Photograph by Smithsonian Institution)

along the roof of the Panda House. A section of that wall was climbable and Ling-Ling discovered this architectural oversight before we did. It was June 24; the weather was unseasonably cool and the pandas had been put outside at the usual time while Tex Rowe and Curley Harper cleaned out their indoor quarters. It was so fine a day that after the animals finished their morning meal, the keepers decided to give them in-out access. At 10:45 A.M., wrote Tex in the logbook, the pandas took advantage of this special privilege and went back outside where they stayed until 1 P.M. It was then that Ling-Ling got up on her squeeze cage and scaled the rock wall up to the top of the fence along the alleyway. There she stood, seven feet off the ground on the catwalk with nothing to keep her from escaping, especially if she made her way to some movable steps leaning against the outside of her paddock wall. The vision of Ling-Ling climbing down the steps and bolting leapt into Curley's mind; he raced around the paddock and shoved the steps away. Tex was right behind and tried to push the panda off the fence into her paddock. Meanwhile, the officer on duty had sent out the alarm to Dr. Reed and he arrived only minutes later, along with several keepers from the Large Mammals Division. This improved the odds, but they were still in favor of the panda on the fence.

"I stared up at her," wrote Dr. Reed later in the *National Geographic*. "She stared down at me. Would she choose the full freedom of the zoo on my side of the fence, or all that lovely bamboo and grass in her own yard?

"Ominously, she slid her forepaws down on my side, apparently preparing to jump. That was too much. I picked up a push broom and batted her firmly on the nose. She swatted back, playing a brand new game called Bat the Broom. I, meanwhile, played Push

In just such a manner, and with a foothold in the cracks between the stones, did Ling-Ling nearly escape. (Photograph by Smithsonian Institution)

the Panda Back. Then she caught the head of the broom and pulled it off the handle."

At about this point in the proceedings a completely uninterested Hsing-Hsing lumbered into his indoor enclosure and Curley locked the door behind him. Meanwhile, Tex Rowe was inside Ling-Ling's paddock whistling and taunting the female. Suddenly she made her move and Tex bolted, saying later that he was "probably the only man in the world who's ever burned rubber" from a pair of boots. She plunged after him into Hsing-Hsing's alleyway. Then began the complicated game of moving pandas. Step 1: Lure Ling-Ling into Hsing-Hsing's den and lock her in. Step 2: Lure Hsing-Hsing out of his enclosure into the alleyway and lock him out. Step 3: Lure Ling-Ling from Hsing-Hsing's den into his enclosure and from there across into her own enclosure, being sure to lock each door behind her.

In all, the entire incident took about a half-hour and as Dr. Reed wrote: "End of game. Score: Keepers 1, Pandas 0."

The quest for the ultimate ball

For all its remarkable achievements, space-age technology had not, by the end of the pandas' first year here, been equal to the task of producing a pandaproof ball. In fact, as the first anniversary neared we felt extremely fortunate that the Panda House itself had proved pandaproof. It almost wasn't.

It was obvious to me, even before the Chinese returned to Peking, that bamboo pots, water pans and a log pile were not going to be enough to keep the pandas busy. At one point in those first hectic days, I managed to get away long enough to make a trip to the toy store and returned in all my innocence with two basketballs. They were regulation American Basketball Association balls, a brilliant red, white and blue, and with the pride of a father at Christmas I put them into the pandas' enclosures. They lasted two days. Ling-Ling rolled hers into a corner, got a grip on it with her great strong jaws, and it was all over. Hsing-Hsing's met a similar fate.

Dr. Robert Sauer, the zoo's pathologist, soon contributed two more basketballs but these were nylon and, cannily, we pumped them up beyond the recommended pressure so that they would be too hard to make a dent in. No dents, we reasoned, meant no place for an incisor tooth to get a purchase. These also lasted for two days.

At this point the Friends of the National Zoo stepped in. They are a group of volunteers who perform a host of essential tasks around the zoo such as staying up nights to watch pregnant animals when their time has just about come, and helping to make scientific observations of various animals including the pandas. Finding the pandas toyless, they paid a local organization engaged in industrial research to produce the ultimate toy. In a few weeks, on July 21, the chief of this firm arrived with two extraordinary balls. Each was made in two sections from extruded, laminated, "space-age" plastic, and the sections were riveted together. They were extremely hard, but leathery, not brittle. Ling-Ling's had two pieces of wood inside it which rattled.

The pandas were outdoors, Ling-Ling resting comfortably in her tub of water. A small group, including

Ling-Ling took immediately to her space-age plastic ball, provided with the compliments of the Friends of the National Zoo. (Photograph by Smithsonian Institution)

Peter Andrews, president of the Friends of the National Zoo, was present on the roof of the Panda House as Mr. Andrews dropped the balls into the paddocks. Ling-Ling's ball landed behind her with a great clattering sound and, startled, she leapt from her bath and rolled over. Seconds later she was chewing the toy and slapping at it. Then she rolled it a ways, held it in her fore-paws, pushed it with her nose, and performed a somer-sault over it. Hsing-Hsing ignored his new toy at first, but eventually began to bat it back and forth. Finally he sat down and simply held it affectionately to his chest. Three months passed and the two plastic balls looked none the worse for wear. (The balls had been guaranteed for one year.) But finally Ling-Ling man-aged to put a small dent in hers and then, over a period of days, worked on this irregularity with her incisors until the space-age plastic succumbed. We removed the ball, as we had the others before, because it was now a hazard to her. I called the manufacturer.

"Impossible!" he cried. "Nothing could break that ball, unless it was heated up a great deal. It must have been heated." I explained that there was no heat in the building. The manufacturer was mystified and still un-believing; he called back three times that same day to ask if it was really true and when I volunteered to show him the toothmarks in the ball he promised, with the determination of General MacArthur leaving the Phil-ippines, "We will build a ball that cannot be broken."

As he went back to work, we gave the female Hsing-Hsing's ball, since she seemed to need the diversion more. But she had learned the technique, and in two days Hsing-Hsing's ball was also in ruins. In a week or so, the manufacturer returned with two more balls made from transparent plastic one-quarter of an inch thick. "This," he said, "is the ultimate ball. Each has been thoroughly tested. I myself have beaten on one with a hammer and it shows no sign of it." The balls were

The ultimate, pandaproof toy after use by the ultimate material-tester. (Photograph by Larry Collins)

rolled into the enclosures with high hopes. Perhaps, at last, we had a pandaproof toy. Two hours later, Ling-Ling swatted her ball against the wall with a resounding thud and knocked a hand-sized piece of plastic out of its spherical surface. The balls were removed and the manufacturer, dazed but still determined, returned once again to the drawing board, with the score: Pandas–2,

Technology–0. By March 1973, he was yet to come up with a new model.

There were other attempts. A toy manufacturer had produced two much larger, three-colored balls of hard plastic, on the theory that they were too large to bite. The pandas chased these balls around their outside enclosures for nearly six months before they learned that if they held the toys in their paws, like fat men with medicine balls, they could then force a tooth into them. A large plastic ring was a great outdoor diversion for a while. This was rolled like a hoop, lain upon, and climbed through, but eventually the pandas grew large enough and strong enough to tear chunks out of it, and it was eventually given to our young orangutan, quickly becoming a much-loved plaything.

Of course, the pandas were not totally dependent on us for diversion. Virtually anything could be turned into one sort of game or another. Large blocks of ice, put inside the enclosures to augment the air-conditioning system on particularly hot days in the summer, became slides. Chunks broken off the corner could, for a moment or two at least, be batted about the enclosure until they wound up as a puddle. Winter brought its own more natural ice, though unfortunately practically no snow. We had a half-inch of snow on February 22, and both animals took to it immediately, rolling around in it (and thereby getting clean). I threw a snowball at Ling-Ling and she ate it. By afternoon the snow had disappeared. On one of the first below-freezing mornings, the pandas were turned outside and Ling-Ling ambled over to her water pan to find it frozen. In minutes she had extracted the ice — in the form of a thick round wheel — and swatted it around her yard like an oversized hockey puck. (On another occasion, there was only a thin film of ice over the water and she put one of her back feet through it to get to the water. It was so cold that the water on her foot began to freeze, attaching pebbles and clods of dirt to her fur — pandas have very hairy paws — and for several minutes she lumbered back and forth, shaking her leg and periodically stopping to look backward through her front legs to see what the disturbance was.)

By January, the toy situation was growing desperate. We had no serviceable toys and both animals were restless — Ling-Ling in particular. When she began biting large hunks of molding from her enclosure door and biting at the walls, I threw caution to the wind and gave each of them an empty tub of the sort we used for planting bamboo. The tubs weighed fifty pounds without the dirt and seemed well enough constructed to last at least a while. Ling-Ling was delighted. She would pick up the fifty-pound tub in her jaws and carry it to the top of her log pile, knock it off, and chase it as it careened around the enclosure. Both pandas took to bashing the tubs against the walls which made a thundering noise that echoed through the Panda House. Then, at 3:30 P.M. on January 16, Ling-Ling picked the tub up in her mouth, swung her head, and hit the three-ply, pandaproof glass, "spider-webbing" the *outer* panel of glass and leaving one ply of glass and one of plastic intact between her and the outside world. That the outer panel of glass was broken by the concussion following the impact and not the inner panel attests to her terrific strength. The tub was quickly removed and we gave her another, larger one filled with dirt, far too heavy to use as a club. Deprived, but undaunted, Ling-Ling proceeded to scratch out the dirt to form a hole that conformed to her behind and thenceforth used the tub as an easy chair. So as her first year in the United States drew to a close, Ling-Ling would often sit comfortably in her tub, her back to the public—the supreme materials-tester, still waiting for the ultimate, panda-proof toy.

The night shift

As the months went by, the pandas paid more and more attention to each other (a subject we will return to in the next chapter) and their mutual games increased in frequency, to the delight of visitors standing on the roof of the Panda House. But there were still days when the pandas played little, refusing even to go outdoors, and slept for much of the day. We realized that on such days they were sleeping off a busy night.

The first to know the pandas fooled around a lot after hours were the zoo policemen on night duty. Each evening after the second meal of the day, the lights in the Panda House are turned off, so that night can fall for the animals just as it does outdoors, and the zoo police take the night watch, sitting in the dark in the public area. Sometimes it gets a little spooky. One night Ling-Ling threw herself against the glass and the

Hsing-Hsing carefully explores his plastic ring. (Photograph by Larry Collins)

officer nearly fell over, so sure was he that she would come through the glass. On another night, after we had resorted to tubs as toys, Ling-Ling shattered the silence by throwing her tub against the glass front of the enclosure. The officer leapt up, gun in hand, he said later that he was going to shoot the lock off the door and "get the hell outta there") and spent a long anxiety-ridden night. We reassured them, of course, about the impermeability of the pandaproof glass, but they were unimpressed, particularly after January 16, the day Ling-Ling "spider-webbed" one pane of her's with her fifty-pound tub. Nor do the police take much comfort from the fact that pandas do not see well at night: The officers still get visions from time to time of Ling-Ling chasing them around the dark public corridor and they know who would win the race.

(In fact, not only do pandas have relatively poor night vision, we believe their eyesight is generally weak. Instead, they appear to rely mainly on smell and hearing, both of which senses are very acute. I have thrown a carrot into Hsing-Hsing's outdoor paddock and watched him walk past it unseeing, only to return and find it after he had detected the scent. Their hearing seems particularly acute. They startle easily from unexpected sharp noises and they are much aware of what the other is doing, almost always having one ear cocked for any activity on the part of the other: even when there are two closed doors between them, they will pay attention if the other begins to move around.)

It turns out that the pandas are active for several periods during almost every night; some nights are more raucous than others and this is evident not only from the pandas' behavior the next day but also from the amount of torn up bamboo and general mess when the keepers show up first thing in the morning. In order to find out more precisely what was going on in these bouts, we have held seven all-night watches, conducted by volunteers from the Friends of the Na-

Hsing-Hsing finds that it makes only a slightly comfortable chair. (Photograph by Larry Collins)

Ling-Ling discovers that a ring is obviously for rolling. (Photograph by Larry Collins)

tional Zoo during the fall of 1972, part of the painstaking schedule of record-keeping and close observations being made by the zoo's scientific staff. In addition to scent-marking (see next chapter), the pandas spend a considerable part of most nighttime hours doing just what they do during daylight — that is, eating and playing.

A few scraps are left in the cages at night and every now and then the pandas will get up for a snack. Hsing-Hsing does most of this between 8 and 10 P.M., while Ling-Ling spends more time eating between 10 P.M. and midnight. But when one panda begins to play, so will the other. The nighttime volunteer observers found that the two pandas, on opposite sides of the wall separating their enclosures, have identical patterns of playing time. They begin in earnest at about ten, reaching a peak at midnight and tapering off until, between the hours of 4 and 6 A.M., they spend most of the time asleep. Just as in their behavior along the wire fence during the day, their nighttime play tends to be in synchrony, a pleasing and hopeful sign of their sociability.

On behalf of the pandas, Larry Collins accepts a perfume company's award: Valentines of the Year. (Photograph by Smithsonian Institution)

6

Scent and Sociability

Every time an animal urinates, it isn't necessarily expressing an opinion.

— TEX ROWE

The commercial response to the pandas was enormous. Stores were filled with pandas, large and small, panda rugs, panda mugs, posters, crewelwork kits, dress fabrics. A Chinese restaurant called "The China Panda" opened up in the Maryland suburbs of Washington. The media were full of pandas. Maxine Cheshire, a Washington gossip columnist, gushed that Henry Kissinger had "been three times to the National Zoo, unannounced, to see Hsing-Hsing and Ling-Ling have their breakfast." Even a hyperintellectual TV critic could find no better metaphor for his disappointment over a new series than to compare it to his disappointment on learning that pandas were raccoons, not bears. (See the next chapter for more of this particular issue.) The drums beat for pandas right through Christmas and showed little sign of slacking off. In January, a perfume manufacturer boarded the bandwagon, proclaiming Hsing-Hsing and Ling-Ling to be the "Valentines of the Year." As part of the ceremonies that accompanied this proclamation, the pandas were given a huge wreath made of red apples, orange carrots and white chrysanthemums which we placed on display alongside the green lacquer crates from China. A few days later a woman visitor grew alarmed when she saw the wreath and anxiously asked Tex Rowe if one of the pandas had died.

As a matter of fact, it is really quite appropriate that a perfume company should honor the pandas because scent is especially important in their lives. They pay close attention to it, and so, therefore, do we.

The mark of a panda

Anyone who owns a dog knows something about scent-marking. Many kinds of animals mark in similar fashion, by urinating. Many animals also have special scent glands with which they perform much the same function. The glands are found in a variety of places on the body depending on what kind of animal it is, but most frequently they are located in the anogenital region. Giant pandas employ both modes. A patch of naked skin around the panda's anogenital region is highly glandular and they generally back up and press this skin against the object to be marked. One of the times these glandular notations are much used is when a female is in heat. We knew this from Desmond Morris' accounts of Chi-Chi and from other sources. Marking is also apparently a means of identifying one's territory, perhaps of making a place familiar and comfortable, rather the way a housewife is uncomfortable in a new home until she has hung her curtains. So we were pleased when, in their first days here, both pandas marked various places and objects in their enclosures. But there was one major surprise in store for us.

On the pandas' seventh day, we noticed Hsing-Hsing back up to a wall, presumably to mark it at tail level. Not at all. After making contact with the wall, he kept right on backing up. His hind legs walked up the wall till he was doing a supported handstand and only then did he mark the wall.

Now this was something new: No one to the best of our knowledge had ever before recorded such a marking posture on the part of a giant panda. Indeed, it took a while to recall any animal that assumed such a posture. Then we remembered that such creatures as civets and mongooses, known zoologically as viverrids, do so (and later in the year a student at the University of Pennsylvania pointed out that the ring-tailed lemur and the brown lemur also are known to adopt this position for marking). We were not quite sure what to make of it, but we were further determined to watch the animals closely and for the time being we took Hsing-Hsing's unusual stance, along with their other more typical marking behavior, as another sign that they were beginning to feel at home.

By December we had spent a great deal of time watching the scent-marking behavior of the pandas. The methods, times, and places were all carefully observed and graphed and some patterns began to emerge. Dr. Devra Kleiman and I presented our findings to the American Association for the Advancement of Science in December. What follows is taken largely from that report.

In addition to rubbing the anogenital area on a wall or other surface or object (which both do) and in addition to Hsing-Hsing's extraordinary handstand, he also employs a position which we call the "leg cock." Finally, he also uses a transitional stage, a partial handstand with one back leg cocked. So he has three distinct positions

Hsing-Hsing executes a "leg cock," marking the wall of his enclosure during one of his regular patrols of its boundaries. (Photograph by Smithsonian Institution)

and can either urinate or use his scent glands, giving him a repertoire of six choices. Finally, both the male and the female will occasionally rub their necks and shoulders over a previously marked place. For Hsing-Hsing, this is especially common after he has urinated.

Hsing-Hsing marks the wall in what is an unusual position: a supported handstand. Most often this posture is associated with his interest in Ling-Ling. (Photograph by Smithsonian Institution)

Not only is Hsing-Hsing more versatile in this business, he is far more assiduous. For example, during the seven consecutive night watches carried out by the volunteers from the Friends of the National Zoological Park, Ling-Ling marked by anogenital rubbing only four times while the male did the same thing over 100 times. (During the night watches, we discovered that the male's pattern of marking followed almost exactly the pattern of play. That is, the peak was between 10 P.M. and midnight.) Why there should be so great a difference between the male and female is not clear nor, in fact, are we really sure why immature animals would behave in such a fashion. Marking is more often the business of adults.

We began to get some clues about Hsing-Hsing's motives by watching him mark under different conditions—indoors and outdoors—and examining the relative frequencies of leg cocks to handstands. Most of the times Hsing-Hsing has been seen marking in a handstand are when he is outdoors—mainly when he and Ling-Ling are playing or at least watching each other. In fact, he nearly always does his handstand against the wire-mesh fence that separates him from her. The night-watch observers found that handstands were also common at night—especially during those times when the two pandas were interacting through the opaque door that separates their cages. So the handstand certainly is a mark of Hsing-Hsing's interest in Ling-Ling: The only time when he does *not* do it very much is during the day when he is indoors, which is the time when the two pandas pay the least attention to each other.

But Hsing-Hsing's handstand is not merely a premature siren call to a prospective lover. We also saw him perform numerous handstands the first few times he was locked outside in his paddock. Mostly, these handstands were directed at the door leading into his quarters and all the rest of his behavior at these times indicated that he was nervous in the new surroundings and wanted to get back to familiar territory.

What the two handstand situations seem to have in common is that Hsing-Hsing is both aroused and thwarted. When he uses this posture he almost invariably marks a barrier between himself and what he wants at the moment. On the other hand, the leg cock is used mainly during his regular patrols of the boundaries of his enclosure and his paddock. So it looks as though the two marking positions arise from different moods and motives. (It is possible that they merely reflect a difference in the degree of arousal. It is possible that Hsing-Hsing's handstands are also related in some way to his usual reluctance, when playing, to turn a headstand into a somersault. These are matters which our continuing observations will explore.)

Whatever the answers to these questions, it does seem clear that nothing arouses Hsing-Hsing so much as Ling-Ling. As the months passed they grew more and more fascinated with each other — Hsing-Hsing more so, but the female was by no means aloof. Just how much more time they had for each other not only was apparent to the casual visitor but was logged and carefully scrutinized by the scientific staff. This is what we found: Of all the hours in the summer months during which the pandas were both outdoors simultaneously, they paid attention to each other a little over 10 per cent of the time. By the late fall, they spent about 45 per cent of their available time interacting. Furthermore, they both spent a great deal more time at the fence whether the other was there or not, though Hsing-Hsing spent twice as much time seeking out Ling-Ling than vice versa.

No coed dormitories

The two pandas obviously enjoy each other's company. Why, then, do we keep them physically separated? A lot of people ask that question and the answer is in two parts. The Japanese learned about the first part in the fall of 1972.

The Ueno Zoo in Tokyo experienced its own P-Day on October 28, 1972, when three Chinese officials arrived with two young pandas, the first ever in Japan. The male, named Kang-Kang, was reported to be two years old when he arrived and to weigh 121 pounds. The female, Lan-Lan, was reported to be four years old and to weigh 194. Still in their crates, the two pandas made their debut before Japanese news media and, in temporary quarters that had formerly housed tigers, they were put on public display six days later on November 4. In the interval, I received the farthest long-distance call in my career. The Japanese zoo official in charge of Kang-Kang and Lan-Lan asked me various details about our experience with pandas — dietary and medical matters mainly. Then he asked if we permitted our pandas to be in physical contact. I told him firmly that we did not, but why did he ask? He replied that on their first day in Tokyo, Kang-Kang and Lan-Lan were put in the same cage.

"What happened?" I asked.

"Very big fight," he replied.

There is no absolute certainty that Ling-Ling and Hsing-Hsing would fight if they were allowed in the same enclosure, but it is highly probable. Furthermore, the difference between fighting and playing might be negligible in regard to the damage the two pandas would do to each other. The keepers and I do not consider Ling-Ling hostile, despite her attempts to take Tex Rowe's leg off in the early days. Certainly she is boisterous, even aggressive—as Hsing-Hsing is becoming as he grows older and larger—but we still consider it playfulness, not hostility, largely because there seems to be something of a game to it. For example, there is a small camera port in one of the doors to each of the pandas' enclosures. Sometimes we open it up, hold a carrot out, and call the panda over. Invariably, in the case of Ling-Ling, she will cross the floor and pass underneath the camera port out of sight, instead of simply coming over and standing up to take our offering. Then with lightning speed out comes a black furry arm through the window: The unwary could easily lose a pound of flesh or be caught in her strong grasp. Having missed, which she always has, she will stretch her forepaw around and, unseeing, rattle the padlock on the outside of the door. It's dangerous, to be sure, but it seems to us to be a game. We sum it up by saying that if they could get a hold of you, they would use you as a toy—with no hard feelings.

The potential for physical damage, then, is one reason to keep the pandas separate. Another, ultimately more important consideration, is the psychological damage that would almost certainly result. Ling-Ling is and will remain for some time the dominant animal of the two. She is larger—though this will have evened out by 1974 —and she is simply more aggressive. This too may change, but were the two pandas to be put together now, whatever else happened, we can be sure that Ling-Ling would take a dominant role which, once established, might never be relinquished. That would provide us with an insuperable obstacle to the tricky business of breeding the animals and, after assuring their well-being, the second great responsibility of the National Zoological Park, so far as Ling-Ling and Hsing-Hsing are concerned, is to do everything possible to achieve a successful mating.

Breeding

The odds certainly are against it. A baby giant panda has never been born outside of China, and the opportunity has existed only twice — once in St. Louis and later in the Chi-Chi — An-An "romance." Previous efforts have been hamstrung by a variety of problems. In several instances supposed pairs turned out to be the same sex. I mentioned Mei-Mei of the Brookfield Zoo in Chicago earlier: another "pair" — Pan-dee and Pan-dah, given to the United States in 1941 by Madame Chiang Kai-Shek — proved to be both females when the "male," Pan-dee, died in New York. The same occurred in London in 1939 when an alleged female, Sung, turned out to be male.

But even when there is a bona fide pair, other problems arise. Perhaps the most elaborate — and frustrating — effort to achieve a mating between pandas occurred in the case of London's Chi-Chi and Moscow's An-An. In October 1960, Chi-Chi went off her food, began bleating a great deal, left scent marks throughout her enclosure and grew very affectionate toward her keepers. She was three and a half years old. For the next three years she went into heat regularly each spring and fall, showing increasing affection for the keepers by pushing her rear end against their legs. But affection became temper, as Desmond and Ramona Morris wrote in *Men and Pandas:*

"When no mate materialized in response to her calls and her scents, her reproductive system went into revolt . . . it began to work overtime . . . 1963 saw two spring periods of heat and two in the autumn. In addition they were more intense and more prolonged. Her spitefulness developed into a 'wicked temper.' Her wanderings through her paddock became more agitated and elaborate."

The last heat of 1963 lasted four months, she began to lose weight and had to be tranquilized. More normal heat periods followed until in March 1966, she was flown to Moscow and met An-An through a wire partition. The two pandas barked at each other and showed great curiosity, so after a few days they were put together. They circled, snarled, and then started to fight. This happened repeatedly and ultimately Chi-Chi returned, unmated, to London. Another try was made, this time with An-An coming to London, but it was equally unsuccessful. One explanation given for these failures is that Chi-Chi had become too dependent upon her human keepers to accept with any relish or interest the attentions of so unfamiliar a beast as another panda. On the assumption that this may be true, the keepers and I are being careful to spend no more time interacting with

111

Ling-Ling and Hsing-Hsing than is absolutely necessary. And we are letting the pandas become familiar with each other gradually and largely at their own speed.

As a part of the familiarization process, we have been letting each panda experience the other's enclosure with all its special panoply of scents and associations. For example, in November we locked Hsing-Hsing into his den and let Ling-Ling through the door that separates the two enclosures. She carefully investigated his entire enclosure and its contents. Hsing-Hsing was immediately aware of her presence in his enclosure. Dave Bryan, who was watching through his den door, saw him take up "a defense posture like that of a cat" and he let out a strange noise as if something was caught in his throat. He continued to make the noise for a half an hour, even after Ling-Ling had gone back to her own quarters. And, as you might have guessed, Ling-Ling's presence — so near and yet so far — was an occasion for a handstand. Aroused and thwarted, he marked the door.

Hopefully, by such strategems, we will overcome whatever problems that might arise between our two charges and one day they will mate. When will that be? Chi-Chi's first heat occurred, as noted before, when she was three and a half. On the other hand, the Chinese who accompanied Ling-Ling and Hsing-Hsing to the United States told me that pandas reach sexual maturity between six and seven years of age. So we don't know for sure and must simply wait. We should have no difficulty recognizing the signs once they develop. The Chinese gave me a list of things to look for. At some point Ling-Ling will begin to lose her appetite. She will become more active, doing a lot of pacing, and she will bleat more than usual. Her genitals will swell and, the Chinese said, she will spend a lot of time lying on her back. She will, in short, be in heat and will be ready. But Hsing-Hsing may not be ready. The Chinese told me that male pandas go through a period of rut and this

Ling-Ling covers her face while a fascinated Hsing-Hsing looks on from the other side of the fence. (Photograph by Smithsonian Institution)

must be in synchrony with the female's heat or nothing will happen except a very big fight. The rut period should also be easily recognized: Hsing-Hsing's activity will increase, he will bleat more often, urinate more often, and his genitals too will swell. He will frequently roll on the ground, according to the Chinese, and I would guess that there will be a lot more scent-marking.

So whenever all this happens all at once will be the time to try a mating, and even then it could well fail. The Chinese themselves have presided over only ten births and perhaps as many as three of these were the result of artificial insemination, according to a French photojournalist, Marc Riband, who visited the Peking Zoo in the mid-1960s. If a mating does take place in Washington, it will be brief—between thirty seconds and about five minutes, the Chinese said, after which the animals should quickly be separated lest a fight start.

If these delicate arrangements finally do take place and are successful, Ling-Ling will enter a pregnancy of about five months. One month prior to giving birth she will begin to lose her appetite and become less active. Her genital area will grow inflamed, becoming redder and swollen a week before giving birth. Her breasts will swell. The day before parturition, she will eat nothing; labor pains will become evident and we will see a yellowish mucous discharge from her genital area. And then a hairless, ratlike creature weighing only 100 grams (5 ounces) may emerge, immediately to become the most famous zoo animal in the history of the United States. Also one of the least observed: The female and its newborn must be kept in strict isolation, the Chinese told us. The young panda's eyes will not open for 75 days. At four months, it will drink water by itself; at five months, it will eat bamboo and be independent.

Until all this happens, however, we have Ling-Ling and Hsing-Hsing and for the time being they are more than enough to keep us busy and amused and, occasionally, puzzled.

Ling-Ling. (Photograph by Stan Wayman)

7

What Is A Panda?

An enigmatic object.
— DESMOND MORRIS

A lot of people ask what giant pandas are. It is a good question. A number of eminent biologists have pondered it for a century and until recently there were two main schools of thought, each convinced its answer was correct and would prevail. Now there are three.

It may seem a little silly for grown men to worry about what would appear to be so simple, even childlike, a question. And even a concern over the identity of pandas may seem a little less wasteful of precious scientific man-hours and research funds than the activities of other eminent biologists who seek to classify such things as obscure tropical beetles or to run down all the relatives of the sunflower and provide them with unpronounceable Latinized names (which in fact are more often than not rather unclassical combinations of Latin and Greek).

But to ask what a panda is or what that beetle is or where this plant came from is not to ask a simple question. Suppose that the answer is that a panda is a bear. Most children may be satisfied because they can then point to a bear at the zoo and say a panda is one of those. But what, after all, is a bear?

Once you start asking questions like these you can find yourself off on a particular adventure which biologists call taxonomy, the classification of living organisms into some kind of systematic arrangement. At its best, taxonomy is a journey out of our normal human-centered world into the almost stupefying richness and variety of living creatures and into the extraordinary story of how they got that way. Now that may sound a bit grand when all that was asked was what a panda is, and a lot of other biologists (particularly experimental ones) would scoff, seeing the preoccupations of their systematic colleagues as little more than stamp-collecting. But, of course, taxonomy is far more than that. To classify anything so complicated as a living organism requires a fairly detailed knowledge of such things as its anatomy, its behavior, its ecological niche, what it eats — and what eats it — its blood type, the fine structure of its nervous system, its evolutionary history, and a host of other details including the same information about a large number of other creatures.

When questioned, and especially when threatened with a loss of research funds, taxonomists can (and do) marshall a long impressive list of highly practical reasons for identifying and naming species of plants and animals. But there is another reason, perhaps a more important one, which a Harvard taxonomist, Howard Ensign Evans, recently expressed in defense of his science when confronted with the statement that what he was doing was not essential: "I doubt if scientific progress has ever resulted from the pursuit of the 'essential.'" Evans went on to quote another scientist who said, "What looks 'important' at any time reflects a consensus based upon what is already known." And if this is true, said Evans, "One could make a strong case for the deliberate pursuit of what seems unimportant and nonessential."

A good reason for taxonomy, then, is simple, straightforward curiosity—the same kind of curiosity that led early man to seek the pattern in the motions of the stars and that leads so many visitors to the National Zoological Park to inquire what a panda is. It is akin to a sense of wonder.

Some things pandas are and are not

Where then does a panda fit into the taxonomic scheme of things? First of all, pandas belong in the phylum chordata, subphylum vertebrata which means that, unlike such animals as worms, clams, sea anemones, and insects, they have a backbone.

Next, a panda is within the class Mammalia, the mammals, which is to say that a panda is not a bird, reptile, amphibian or fish. Instead, it is characterized by milk glands with which it feeds its young and it has hair or fur on its body.

Among the mammals, pandas are in what taxonomists call, with military flair, the cohort Ferrungulata and that means they are *not* very closely related to whales and dolphins, or rabbits and rodents, or moles, monkeys or anteaters. Ferrungulata includes carnivores and hoofed mammals together with some isolated types such as the elephants and sea cows, and many other forms now extinct.

And indeed pandas are considered to be in the order Carnivora, meaning meat-eating mammals (never mind that wild pandas eat mostly bamboo; we will return to that later).

Within the order Carnivora, there are marine creatures

like walruses and seals (the pinnipeds, meaning fin-footed) and a lot of land-living carnivores which comprise the suborder Fissipedia. Fissipedia means paw-footed and there are two kinds or superfamilies. One of these includes hyenas and cats and the other, the super-family Canoidea, includes dogs, bears, raccoons and such animals as weasels and skunks. And it is here, of course, that all the trouble starts.

The bears are in one family called Ursidae; the raccoons, along with coatis and kinkajous from South America are in the family Procyonidae. In which of these two families do the pandas belong? Ursidae or Procyonidae?

Bears versus raccoons

The bear-raccoon controversy began as soon as Westerners saw the giant panda. (It is said that the Chinese have known of these animals for nearly four thousand years and kept them in zoos as early as the eleventh century. In those days the Chinese referred to pandas as white bears.) The first Westerner to see a giant panda was Père David, a French missionary with the bent of a naturalist, who had been sent into the wild rugged country of western China in the 1860s. He, like the Chinese, considered the giant panda to be a bear and sent skins and skulls to a Parisian zoologist named Alphonse Milne-Edwards who promptly proclaimed the panda to be closer to a raccoon.

The question, then as now, was complicated by the fact that there are two kinds of pandas, the giant panda and the lesser panda, a much smaller, reddish-brown

A lesser (or red) panda, one of the two adults at the National Zoological Park, looks much like a raccoon. (Photograph by Smithsonian Institution)

animal with a ringed tail which looks, even on first glance, something like a raccoon. Known to European zoologists a half-century before the giant panda, this smaller creature is also found in western China where giant pandas occur, but its range is considerably greater, extending into northern Burma and northern India. The lesser panda prefers high altitudes, between 3,000 feet and 15,000 feet, and reportedly it also eats bamboo as its main diet. Finally, on closer examination of much of its anatomy, the lesser panda has much in common with the raccoons, coatis and kinkajous.

When Milne-Edwards saw Père David's specimen he found such strong similarities between the teeth and bones of both kinds of pandas that he decided the two belonged together next to, if not among, the raccoons. Over the next hundred years, the bear school and the raccoon school argued back and forth in learned journals and the panda's taxonomic name has accordingly changed some ten times.

Here is a partial listing of features each side has claimed at one time or another as evidence for its view:

Raccoonlike features	*Bearlike features*
Teeth	Bones
Bones	Brain
Skull	Blood type
Viscera	"Sixth claw"
"Sixth claw"	Musculature
Small intestine	Respiration
Stomach	
Liver	
Genitals	

The trick here of course is not to add up the features and give the award to whichever family has the longest list. These are almost all matters of judgment—for example, just *how* bearlike is the musculature of the panda? Enough to outweigh its *un*bearlike teeth? And, as can be seen from the overlap on the abbreviated list above, the judges do not agree even about the bearlikeness of the bones.

In 1964, Dwight D. Davis of the University of Chicago sought to clear the air with a definitive monograph in which he stated that "every morphological [i.e., anatomical] feature examined indicates that the giant panda is nothing more than a specialized bear." He could also point to tests that had been run on the blood of giant pandas, raccoons, polar bears, and other carnivores eight years earlier. These showed the panda much closer to bears than raccoons. Here was a *numerical* index, not a matter of opinion. Nonetheless, the raccoon school rose up to say that Davis overstated the anatomical case greatly and that more sophisticated serological tests were needed.

Another consideration is that there is more to an animal than its structure. Recently, taxonomists have been adding behavioral information to their mix of features on the theory that behavior too is inherited and comparable behavior would indicate that two kinds of animals were closely related. So far, for pandas, the behavioral data is of a negative sort only and not helpful to the bear school. In the 1960s, Desmond Morris, then Curator of Mammals at the London Zoo, made sound spectrograms of Chi-Chi's vocalizations and confirmed her keeper's insight—that is, the giant pandas

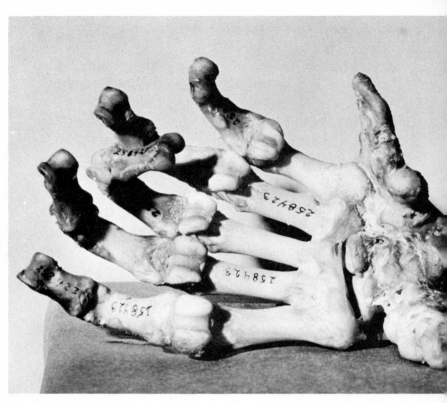

What looks like a thumb in this skeletal panda hand is an elongated wristbone, known as the "sixth claw." It makes grasping possible, much like a thumb. See frontispiece to this chapter to see how Ling-Ling's "hand" looks. (Photograph by *National Geographic*)

bleat, they do not roar like bears. Furthermore, their general scent-marking behavior (wherein they press the glands of their anogenital region to spots they wish to mark) is considered unbearlike, as in fact is the structure of this part of their anatomy. Indeed the peculiar scent-marking behavior of Hsing-Hsing (his supported handstand) is unknown among bears *and* raccoons.

The big problem all along for the bear school has

been to explain how the giant panda could have descended from bears and ended up so similar in many features to the clearly raccoonlike lesser panda. In other words, if the giant panda is a bear, it isn't closely related to the lesser panda. Proponents of the bear theory say that it is not impossible for two distinct and unrelated animals to have converged in some particulars. Both pandas have teeth and jaws nicely designed for eating bamboo and the reason might be just that: As their unrelated ancestors took independently to eating bamboo, their teeth would have developed over many generations into the same kind of equipment. Bear proponents have found this more compelling than the raccoon school's suggestion that gigantism is not at all uncommon, that in many animal groups one or more species have evolved into huge beasts with the intermediate stages dying out.

Of course, all of this argument is over evolution: How best to explain the way the giant panda evolved from which ancestors and when, as well as where. This is what is really meant by "relatedness" of two kinds of animals and it is what the binominal system of nomenclature, the two Latinized names, seeks to summarize.

The formal name of the giant panda has remained relatively stable in recent years, while the argument over its proper family has remained in doubt. The name is *Ailuropoda melanoleuca. Ailuropoda* means cat-footed and there is no other animal in this genus except the large black and white kind — *melanoleuca.* (The lesser pandas constitute a separate genus and species: *Ailurus fulgens* which, just to make things a little more confusing, means fire-colored cat.)

So, the taxonomic scheme can be filled in for the giant panda, except for one crucial blank—the family—which still leaves us without an answer to the original question, what is a panda?

Phylum	Chordata
Subphylum	Vertebrata
Class	Mammalia
Cohort	Ferrungulata
Order	Carnivora
Suborder	Fissipedia
Superfamily	Canoidea
Family	?
Genus	*Ailuropoda*
Species	*melanoleuca*

It is time to look backward and see where all these carnivorous groups came from to see what light that sheds. Here, as in modern zoological studies, one is hampered by the need for a lot of guesswork and judgment.

Becoming carnivorous

As a matter of fact, carnivores evolved twice. The first batch were all failures (if you can say that fifteen million years of existence means failure and your only criterion of success is existence today).

Sometime about 60 million years ago there was a small forest-dwelling mammal that looked something like a weasel. It had claws on slender limbs and probably climbed trees for food and protection. During the next 30 million years these small creatures gave rise to various kinds of animals as they moved into new habitats, and the slow statistical business of natural selection began to weed out those groups incapable of coping with the new problems of a changed environment. Paleontologists call all of these creatures creodonts. Many remained small, like weasels; others grew large, filling much the same niche as bears do today. These larger ones tended to have blunt cheek teeth like the omnivorous bears of today. (It is true that your *teeth*, at least, are what you eat.) Other creodonts became predators comparable in their roles—and their sharp cheek teeth —to the fast-moving cats and wolves of today. One of these highly predatory creodonts, a hyenalike animal, survived all the others, which had become extinct by the end of the Eocene epoch about 36 million years ago. The *Hyaenadon* lasted another ten million years before it finally succumbed as well. A large and varied group of animals, playing most of the roles we know as the roles of modern carnivores, had begun and ended, leaving no descendants. Why?

The bet had been hedged, almost 60 million years ago, when the early creodonts were eking out their wary, primitive existence in the forests. In fact, other small weasel-like, forest-dwelling animals called miacids had evolved from an ancestor common with creodonts. The miacids had proportionately larger brains and cheek teeth that were further forward in their jaws like today's carnivores. Indeed, the miacids are considered the direct ancestors of all of today's carnivores.

By about 35 million years ago, some of the miacids had developed longer legs for running, sharper cheek teeth for shearing off hunks of flesh, and a larger brain case. These were the earliest dogs, the canids. Except for what several thousand years of human breeders have accomplished, many of these early canids were much like the canids of today—our wolves, foxes and dogs. At about the same time that the canids came into being, various other miacid strains were taking other routes. One led to the family which includes our modern weasels, minks, skunks and others.

Another miacid strain, without changing very much over the millennia, evolved into the modern civets, cat-like creatures in some respects, the most well-known of which is the snake-killing mongoose. Some ten to fifteen million years after this family (called Viverridae) arose, it in turn gave rise to a larger-skulled, longer-legged creature that resulted in the hyena. But, before that, again in that lively time when the canids were developing and the viverrids were getting under way, one viverrid strain branched off to become in time the most fully equipped and best designed meat-eating predators we know: the cats.

It is likely that the competition from the early canids, cats and other carnivores, with their greater intelligence and capabilities, drove the creodonts out of their niches and into oblivion. In nature, no two kinds of animals can long play the same role on the same stage.

Along about 25 million years ago, some of these canid carnivores diverged away from chasing and killing prey to a different way of life. The forepaws of the new strain were more like hands, the limbs flexible for climbing. Their cheek teeth became blunt, more suitable for chewing other food besides meat—practically any food they could find as they darted around in rocks or the branches of trees. These, the procyonids, were the early ancestors of the raccoons. They originated in North America and invaded South America as the fluctuating seas and the isthmus of what is now Panama permitted. And one branch of procyonids apparently took the opposite route, heading north over the now submerged Bering Straits into Asia. Ultimately this progenitor of the lesser panda reached as far as England, where its fossils have been discovered, but later some yet unknown series of events caused its range to shrink back to the Himalayan region.

A few million years after the procyonids had begun to exploit the rocks and trees, some of the canids began to evolve into much larger animals. As the skeleton grew heavier and the skull more massive, the cheek teeth also lost their shearing function and became blunt and elongated. The tail became shorter, the legs heavier. They gradually lost the habit of pursuing their prey. They became bears, omnivorous, intelligent, adaptable. Originating also in the Northern Hemisphere, they extended their range southward into southern Asia and South America, though not Africa.

And here we are again. Did the giant panda evolve from the wide-ranging ancestors of the lesser panda or from the more recently arrived and equally cosmopolitan bears?

The conservatives have it—for now

In biology the opposite of conservative is not liberal but advanced. Conservative in such a context means about the same as primitive. While evolution proceeds at different rates among animals (think of how long a clam has been just a clam), it also can proceed at varying rates as far as the parts of an animal are concerned. In other words, an animal can have conservative, or primitive, elements and advanced elements all in the same body. The early procyonids were primitive in most features compared to today's raccoon. Most of the features of a bear are advances on those of the early canids and, for that matter, modern dogs. But most features of the dog, except for its brain, its teeth, and its legs, are not much advanced over the early miacids. So perhaps the way to answer the confusing matter of the giant panda is to seek out important features and decide if they are conservative or advanced. This is what Dr. John Eisenberg, Resident Scientist of the National Zoo, and Dr. Henry Setzer of the Smithsonian Institution's National Museum of Natural History attempted in a thorough review of panda taxonomy and the fossil record completed just before Ling-Ling and Hsing-Hsing arrived in the United States.

In the business of surviving or being extinct, the critical element is reproduction, so it is not unreasonable to look carefully at the reproductive system of an animal. Both the lesser and the giant panda have "glandular areas in association with the genitalia (which) are neither canidlike nor ursidlike," according to the Smithsonian scientists. Nor is the marking behavior like bears or canids. And, the two scientists said, "the penis structure is conservative and more nearly reminiscent of viverrid carnivores and cats than either canids or ursids." This convinced them that the ancestors or ancestor of both pandas "differentiated very early from the primitive miacid stock and have retained conservative features with respect to these structures."

Thus, it would appear that the beginning of the pandas lay somewhere far back in the Miocene, *long* before one line of canids had started to become bears. Eisenberg and Setzer also pointed to a Spanish fossil called *Schlossericyon* from Miocene times which could well have been the common ancestor for both the lesser and giant panda. They suggest, then, that both pandas be placed in a separate family called Ailuridae, reserving the closely related family Procyonidae for those creatures that radiated throughout the New World—resulting in today's raccoons, coatis and kinkajous. When the Chinese arrived with Ling-Ling and Hsing-Hsing, we discovered that the Chinese too had come to the similar conclusions and had placed both pandas in a separate family they call Ailuropodidae. So the answer to the question—is a panda a bear or a raccoon?—is: Neither. It's a panda.

Becoming a panda

The rest—all the details of panda evolution—is mainly guesswork. One can reasonably imagine a series of events, taking place over an unimaginably long period of time over an unknowable number of generations, that went something like this:

Some 30 or 35 million years ago the miacids gave rise to the earliest progenitors of what we now think of as dogs. In a number of "experiments"—that is, mindless combinations of genetic aberrations and new environments — some of these relatively intelligent beasts began to adapt to a tree-dwelling way of life, reversing their long-legged hunting trend and becoming omnivorous as had others before them. By approximately 25 million years ago, some of these creatures were on their precarious way to becoming raccoons and other procyonids. Some of these creatures, however, halted in some respects, becoming something like the lesser pandas of today and spreading (as they went through the continuing process of natural redesign) across the Bering Straits into Asia and Europe. But, for reasons unclear, their conservative approach was not adequate to a changing and probably more competitive world. They shrank back in range, still adapting but this time to a peculiar dietary niche — bamboo — and to a cold, remote, less populated area — the Himalayas.

In the process, even this conservative strain had been sending forth experimental versions — larger versions. Indeed, fossil pandas have been found that were larger than the giant pandas of today. Again, this did not happen overnight. Lesser panda-like animals were exploiting the relatively predator-free canopy of bamboo-conifer forests. Larger ones presumably developed with heavier jaws, capable of eating more fulsome stalks. The hunting life of the carnivore had already long ceased to be necessary — or possible — but size would bring too great a body weight to live in the trees, and on the ground were other competitors, predators capable of attacking and defeating a relatively slow-moving, overlarge lesser panda. There would have been a premium on rapid development of size — great size, great large jaws capable of inflicting a death-dealing bite, as well as able to snap a thick bamboo stalk. It is quite possible that such a large animal would find a statistical advantage in showing up clearly to possible predators so that attacks and exhausting fights would be minimized. As the generations of giant versions grew more gigantic, the black markings of a lesser panda-like animal might have become large black patches around the eyes and on the shoulders and legs meaning: Keep clear.

Intermediate sizes — too big to ply the upper branches, not big enough to threaten predators, too big and cumbersome to escape, not big enough to turn and fight successfully — might well have survived in easier times but fallen prey in a very final sense to the burgeoning competition on the ground from a rapidly proliferating variety of carnivores. Only, perhaps, the larger ones, relegated by a peculiar ability to live in a fairly unique, cold mountainous habitat where there were few competitors and plenty of bamboo, would survive, there to make an increasingly specialized, increasingly local kind of life.

Perhaps.

It all remains a series of guesses, an attempt to see a plausible series of events in a long and ultimately unknowable history. And as John Eisenberg and Henry Setzer wrote in their taxonomic review, "A classification system is at best a compromise between uniting related groups and indicating the divergence of groups." We may never have a wholly satisfactory notion of what, exactly, a panda is — or how it reached its present state.

Raccoon

Procyonidae

Giant Panda

Lesser Panda

Ailuropodidae

NOW

25 MILLION YEARS AGO

36 MILLION YEARS AGO

M

How some carnivores may be related. (Photographs by Smithsonian Institution)

Bear

Wolf

Leopard

Ursidae

Canidae

Felidae

Viverridae

Mongoose

DS

We on the staff and among the volunteers who are engaged (and that is the word for it) in working with Ling-Ling and Hsing-Hsing, will continue to keep a close record of all of their activities — their daily appetite, the amount of time spent feeding, eating, sleeping, every scrap of their behavior. These two pandas amount to about 10 per cent of all the living evidence ever available to Western science on the question of what a panda is and, unbeknownst to them, they will probably go a long way to providing a more precise answer. We also have another source of insight.

About 500 yards down the sloping blacktop walk from the Panda House is a fenced-in circle of grass out of which rises a sycamore tree. Thousands of visitors walk past on their way to see the pandas and the elephants or down to the Apes and Small Mammals House. Many of these visitors fail to look up into the branches of this sycamore tree where a pair of adult lesser pandas named Rishi and Mara quietly go about their business. They do very well in the zoo. In the midst of the wind and rain of hurricane Agnes on June 21, 1972, Mara produced twins in a hole in the tree.

The staff at the zoo is beginning to pay more attention to this unpretentious circle of grass these days for here too lies (or rather climbs) part of the answer to the question, what is a panda? Mike Roberts and Ron Crombie, the lesser pandas' keepers have been gathering a great deal of data on their charges whom — with appropriate pride — they find more interesting behaviorally than the giant pandas. Behavioral observations, blood tests, sound spectographs — all of these will be done on both groups of pandas in the National Zoo. But

Born during a hurricane at the National Zoological Park, two young lesser pandas explore a box. (Photograph by Smithsonian Institution)

even without the sophisticated training and elaborate techniques of the zoologist, any visitor may stroll from the Panda House to the sycamore tree and back and have plenty of material to ponder for himself or herself the enigmatic business of being a panda.

Director Theodore Reed watches Ling-Ling while Ling-Ling watches Dr. Reed. (Photograph by *National Geographic*)

8

Outsmarting Pandas

Any animal that can invent so many games for itself is not dumb.

— CURLEY HARPER

Biologists consider it a cardinal sin to be anthropo-morphic — that is, to attribute to a beast motives or mental qualities that are human. With good reason the biologists claim it to be highly unlikely that, say, a lizard or even your pet dog thinks much the way you do. In their campaign to stamp out anthropomorphism, biologists have not been helped in the least by many children's books and all Walt Disney animal movies. And Ling-Ling and Hsing-Hsing will probably make matters worse, because pandas cry out for anthropo-morphisms (none of which, hopefully, have crept into this book without being clearly identified as such). Simply to look into the slanted, almond-shaped black eyes of Ling-Ling or of Hsing-Hsing is to feel that there is more going on inside that big head than the dim, protothoughts of a mere beast.

Just how smart *is* a giant panda? And what kind of intelligence does it possess? Those are, in fact, ques-tions for which no precise answers exist and which there is probably no way of answering precisely. Given the paucity of giant pandas, not to mention other fore-seeable complications, no one has ever run any psycho-logical test on them. In fact, judgments about any ani-mal's intelligence are very risky altogether, among other reasons because, being human, we don't really know what we mean by an animal's intelligence.

No one has ever accused raccoons or bears of being stupid, so, since pandas are related (albeit distantly), one might say there is reason to believe they are not stupid either. But not only is that another risky assumption, it also doesn't take us very far. In the absence of anything concrete, it is best to go on impressions.

One authority's impressions convinced him that the panda "is an extremely stupid beast . . . not alert . . . dull and primitive in temperament." This was Mr. William G. Sheldon who is one of the few men from the West to have ever observed giant pandas in the wild. His observations were made while on a collecting trip for the American Museum of Natural History in 1934, and he was amazed to find that on several occasions giant pandas showed virtually no sign of alarm or even interest when the collectors' dogs were chasing them and bullets were whistling past them. Having no serious predators except man and having limitless and ready supply of bamboo to eat, the giant panda, Mr. Sheldon concluded, had little need of brains. At least, so he had indicated in 1937 in the *Journal of Mammalogy*, and when I read his account in the summer of 1972 I could hardly wait to tell him of the zoo visitors who ask the keepers and me how long it took us to train our pandas to do so many tricks with their plastic toys. And Mr. Sheldon very graciously wrote me that his early opinion and statements were dogmatic and those of a young man—that trouble-free wild pandas are simply unwary—after I told him a little story about a very different kind of giant panda than the dull animals he had encountered in the wild. (On March 20, Mr. Sheldon visited Hsing-Hsing and Ling-Ling at the

National Zoological Park and he observed two very alert and rambunctious pandas playing in their outdoor paddocks.)

The door game

Not long after our pandas' arrival there was an afternoon reception in the Panda House for several senators and congressmen, the occasion being a forthcoming visit by Representatives Gerald Ford and Hale Boggs to Peking. About a half-hour before the reception was to start, Curley Harper and I arrived to replace the potted bamboo which Ling-Ling had, of course, destroyed during the day. We naturally wanted things looking fresh and shipshape for so distinguished an audience.

This was only a few weeks after we had learned that it was best for Ling-Ling to be locked in her den when we had to work in her enclosure. Even in such a short period of time, however, she had learned what to expect from us and, as it turned out, she had no intention of going into her den, fresh bamboo and the United States Congress notwithstanding. When we arrived she was rolling around and standing on her head; by the time we reached the controls for the shift door to her den, she was lying close to the doorway on her back watching us. As we began to close the door, she casually rolled her head into the track. On our next attempt, she merely lifted one of her back paws and braced the door open.

This went on for several minutes. The congressmen were due shortly and Ling-Ling's enclosure was a disreputable shambles of torn up bamboo. I began to sweat. We went for some honey bread — it was still the time when this was a foolproof bribe — and threw a piece into her den. She lay on her back near the doorway and looked at it for several seconds. Then she looked at us. And, to our utter frustration, there she stayed. All in all, this door game went on for twenty minutes until I quit, and the congressmen saw Ling-Ling *au naturel*.

The Tub Game

There is also the tub game; in fact, there are several. One of them went like this. On one occasion, when Ling-Ling was in her paddock, she tipped her empty tub over on its side, backed up and somersaulted directly at the tub, knocking it back on its bottom. She then turned the tub on its side again, moved away a different distance than before and tried again, with the same results. After four or five attempts, somersaulting from different distances and different angles, she succeeded in having her rear end hit the tub in just the right spot so that the tub righted itself with her sitting inside, her forelegs resting on the rim like an old granny sitting in a favorite armchair.

"It appeared to me," says Tex Rowe who observed this event, "that she had a definite end in mind when she first turned the tub onto its side." And having once learned the knack from trial and error, she could (until she grew too large for the tub) repeat the trick at will.

We also have to be very careful about putting anything large into her paddock unless it is anchored. I've

Ling-Ling rolls her water tub, having first knocked it over to empty out the water. (Photograph by Larry Collins)

watched her haul such items as her old bathing tub, her plastic ring, an aluminum beer keg and a plastic ball over to the fence and stand on them. This gives her additional height and puts her closer to the top.

And so it goes. Both pandas now know the techniques. Almost everyday, in one situation or another, the question arises: Who will outsmart whom? So far we are ahead. . . .

Appendix A

Common Questions About Pandas

Here is some ready reference information on giant pandas, organized into question-and-answer form. The questions (in no particular order) include those most commonly asked by zoo visitors as well as a few not often asked. This section is based on materials prepared by the public information office of the National Zoological Park and by the Friends of the National Zoo.

Where Do Giant Pandas Come From?

China, in the central northern parts of Szechuan Province and the southern end of Kansu Province. They live in dense bamboo and coniferous forests at altitudes from 5,000 to 10,000 feet. The mountains are shrouded in heavy clouds, there are torrential rains and dense mists the year round. Temperature is cold and snow lies on the ground until June. In these huge mountains there are deep gorges with rushing water and foaming rapids.

What is the Scientific Name?

Ailuropoda melanoleuca

How Big Are They?

Full grown they will weigh 300 pounds and measure six feet from the tip of the nose to the end of the little stumplike tail. About the size of an American black bear.

What Do They Eat in the Wild?

Their staple diet is various types of bamboo, but they also eat flowers, vines, tufted grass and some animal matter. Sometimes they raid farmers' crops for green corn. Honey, when they can find it, is a great treat.

How Do They Eat?

With the use of specialized forefeet, the giant panda can grasp food with precision and carry it to the mouth. This thumblike specialization is an elongated wristbone covered with a tough, fleshy pad. (See *How to eat bamboo* in chapter 3.)

Special Adaptations?

Mighty molars for chewing bamboo, an esophagus with a horny lining, a thick-walled, muscular, almost gizzardlike stomach, a short intestine, and an extended wristbone on each forepaw that acts somewhat like a thumb.

Are They Rare?

The number of giant pandas living in the wild is unknown. According to some explorers they are fairly plentiful, while others say they are only moderately so. They are considered rare but not in danger of extinction. The Chinese are very proud of these animals and they are strictly protected by the laws of the People's Republic of China.

Do Pandas Live in Groups?

In the wild, they are usually solitary animals and pair up only during the breeding season which lasts for a month in the spring and again in the fall. Occasionally, a mother and her young will be seen together. (See *Chinese interpretations in* chapter 2.)

What Is Their History?

Although the Chinese have known about them for 4,000 years, the giant panda was not known to the rest of the world until 1869 when a Jesuit missionary, Père Armand David, reported their existence. The first live giant panda taken out of China was Su-Lin, a male, which was purchased for the Brookfield Zoo in Chicago in 1937.

What Is the Gestation Period?

Between 118 and 168 days.

How Many Young Are Born at a Time?

Usually one but occasionally twins and rarely triplets. (See chapter 2.)

How Big Is a Newborn Baby Giant Panda?

Very small, weighing only five ounces. (See *Chinese interpretations* in chapter 2 and *Breeding* in chapter 6.)

Where Do They Sleep?

Their favorite spots are at the bottom of trees, under dead stumps, and in crevices of ledges. Sometimes they make a nest of bamboo stalks. They are active in the morning and again in the evening, sleeping or resting during the day and in the middle of the night.

Can They Climb Trees?

The young ones frequently do and adults do once in a while, but the adults are clumsy climbers.

Can They Walk on Their Hind Legs?

They often push themselves up into a standing position against a vertical surface, but they have never been seen walking on their hind legs as some bears do.

153

Do They Make a Noise?

Their sounds are like coughs or bleats.

Is a Giant Panda a Bear or a Raccoon?

Some scientists believe they are closest to bears, others believe they are part of the same family as raccoons. The Chinese and scientists at the Smithsonian Institution and the National Zoological Park say neither. This is so interesting a question that we devoted an entire chapter (chapter 7) to it.

When Are Ling-Ling and Hsing-Hsing Most Active?

During feeding times at 9:30 A.M. and 4 P.M. (winter hours), or 10:00 A.M. and 4:30 P.M. (summer hours), and when they are outdoors, usually before their breakfast. Also they are active at night. (See *The night shift* in chapter 5.) In the wild, pandas are reported to be crepuscular; that is, rather than being strictly nocturnal or strictly diurnal, they are active around dawn and dusk and sleep during the middle of the day.

When Were Ling-Ling and Hsing-Hsing Born?

Ling-Ling was born in the fall of 1970; Hsing-Hsing in the spring of 1971. (See *Chinese interpretations* in chapter 2.)

What Do Ling-Ling and Hsing-Hsing Eat?

See chapter 3 and Appendix B.

When Will They Be Allowed to Be Together?

Not until they have reached breeding age which might be as early as three and a half years of age but might not be until they are six years old. (See *Breeding* in chapter 6.)

What Do Their Names Mean?

Ling-Ling means cute little girl. Hsing-Hsing means bright star.

Appendix B

Diets for Ling-Ling and Hsing-Hsing

The pandas' first meal in the National Zoological Park, prepared by Mr. Yang of the Peking Zoo, was as follows:

Ling-Ling

Rice gruel:
> $\frac{1}{2}$ kilogram of dry rice, brought to a boil and simmered 20 minutes
>
> 75 grams of powdered milk
>
> 25 grams of sugar
>
> 5 grams of bone meal

1 softball-sized ball of corn meal

400 grams of apples

150 grams of carrots

Hsing-Hsing

Rice gruel:
> as above except $\frac{1}{4}$ kilogram of rice was used

$\frac{1}{2}$ ball of corn meal

600 grams of apples

By July, both pandas' diets had been increased, as follows:

Ling-Ling

A.M.

3 cups rice gruel (see below)

4 apples

2 sweet potatoes

6 carrots

1 large Milk-bone (for *large* dogs!)

1 handful of kale
5 pounds of cut bamboo

Rice gruel:
      3 cups (after cooking) rice
      1 teaspoon Vidalyn M multivitamin drops
      2 tablespoons Purvinal
      1 teaspoon iodized salt
      4 tablespoons sugar
      $\frac{1}{4}$ can ZuPreem Feline diet

P.M.
Same as above.

Hsing-Hsing

A.M.
Rice gruel:
      2 cups rice (before cooking)
      1 teaspoon Vidalyn M multivitamin drops
      1 tablespoon Purvinal
      $\frac{1}{2}$ teaspoon iodized salt
      4 tablespoons sugar
      $\frac{1}{4}$ can ZuPreem Feline diet

5 apples
5 carrots
1 handful of kale
2 sweet potatoes
1 large Milk-bone
3 pounds of cut bamboo

P.M.
Same as above.

As of March 1973, the following diet was fed each animal each day:

Breakfast (9:30 A.M.)

3 pounds (approximately) fruit and vegetables including: apples, carrots, and cooked sweet potatoes

3½ pounds (approximately) rice gruel consisting of: 3 cups rice (cooked), 2 tablespoons Purvinal (a mineral-vitamin supplement), 1 teaspoon Vidalyn M multivitamin drops, 2 tablespoons honey and 2 cups (approx.) water

¼ can ZuPreem feline diet

1 Milk-bone

6 pounds Bamboo (cut)

Lunch (12:30 P.M.)

3 pounds apples and carrots

Supper (4 P.M.)

Same as breakfast

In addition: Both animals browse on bamboo and graze on the grass when in their outdoor paddocks. Occasionally they are given a bread and honey sandwich as a treat.

Index